Praise for *Midsummer Count*

"Robin Becker wonders within and across time for the stray phenomena of connection, crafting poems that make legible something vital but forgotten between us. *Midsummer Count* is a celebration of Becker's extraordinary adeptness at drawing the unsung more dearly and clearly inside a sacred whole, and of her ongoing attunement to the daily mysteries that would bring us into greater communion with ourselves and with each other. Bless Robin Becker."—GEFFREY DAVIS, author of *One Wild Word Away: Poems*

"As 'the whole wrecked world/slides into tomorrow,' Robin Becker's art seeks beauty but does not look away from its opposite. Becker's poems use memorable figuration (compassion is a horse, lies are carpenter bees), painterly detail, and psychological insight, infused with the poet's inimitable warmth and wit. Truths about women's lives (Muriel Rukeyser's plea) shine like silver in this book."—NATASHA SAJÉ, author of *The Future Will Call You Something Else: Poems*

"Robin Becker's voice as a poet is unique. It is complex. There's a rasp in it, but also a sweet viola. She is very American, and a world traveler. She addresses our speeding time and vast space with intelligence, passion, and nuance. She could eat ham on rye, except that she's a Jew who celebrates 'the sounds of Yiddish.' Her poems are wonderfully full of animals, especially horses. Her family portraits are abloom with vitality and suffering—and humor, as in this one of her father as 'the self-inventing Polish immigrant's / son, transformed / by American tools into Errol Flynn.' Tracking the glamor and ordinariness of queerness, she dreams herself 'a handsome specimen in bright plumage / recognizable on the wing.' You have to love a poet who says 'Connecticut is a long / aquamarine word,' and who is deeply aware that 'Hands go to the heart to acknowledge / life as blessed.' Reader, take this ride with Robin Becker's career and be illuminated, enlivened, and enriched."—ALICIA OSTRIKER, author of *The Holy & Broken Bliss*

"Robin Becker is one of our essential poets. She is a born storyteller, and in this legacy book she tells the story of her life, her heartbreaks along the way, increasing her heart-breaking powers. Yet her story does not end with her sorrows, for it is leavened by grace and love and the possibility of reaching beyond obstacles and fear to find, in life and in art, places of perfect affection."—WESLEY MCNAIR, author of *Late Wonders: New and Selected Poems*

"For decades, and certainly since her Lambda Literary Award–winning *All-American Girl*, Robin Becker has inspired and instructed us on how to be the portrait of the artist as a Jewish woman, a lesbian, a sister, a daughter, a lover, a traveler, and a teacher of the craft of poetry. With grace and grit, the poems that span her career now reside together in one volume to magnify their mastery and thematic conversations over time."—SANDRA YANNONE, author of *The Glass Studio*

Praise for Previous Books by Robin Becker

The Black Bear Inside Me
"These poems bear the richness of rural community—horses, dogs, fields, crops, flowers, neighbors—in their fullness of season, celebration, death, and grief. Their homespun appeal is located in a rural landscape populated with characters-as-comrades for whom the writer shows great affection and bonding . . . Becker's unique gift is her generous attention to and comfort with the diversity of others—human and non-human, fauna and flora, music and dance, neighbor and family."—RISA DENENBERG, *The Rumpus*

"Like Becker's entire body of work, *The Black Bear Inside Me* is fundamentally about grieving and living on. Grief is both explicit and implicit, written and inferred. Becker mourns a science teacher who died at the age of ninety-eight in a beautiful elegy. The poem, dedicated to Maria D. Peters travels the world through natural history, ending with Peters's father begging a Jewish scientist to leave Germany in 1935. In another poem, a mother is mourned in the 'whir' of a hummingbird. . . . Each poem maps the complex spaces of loss and memory, illuminating the vitality of loss in defining the human condition."—JULIE ENZER, *The Lambda Literary Review*

Tiger Heron
"In this collection, beloved parents face illness and death; daughters grieve; friends, lovers, and cityscapes strain, crumble, and seek restoration; rescue dogs blend adoration with ingrained fear of brutal pasts; and rainforests and coral reefs sparkle with dying beauty. Becker's vision of our relationships with each other and the natural world is complex, but the writing is limpid, sculpted. She never turns away from the ugliness and contradictions of the human experience, but gives hope through her willingness to let human suffering live on the same page as amazingly varied birds and reptiles."—CATHERINE WALD, *Friends Journal*

Domain of Perfect Affection
"For thirty years, Robin Becker has been tracking a passion for something not fully manifest except in moments of uttering its name: perfect affection. Her tones may change dramatically from page to page. This is why with Becker, there are her poems, and then there are her books. . . . Her work is noted for its receptivity to the personal, an affectionate attention to the animal world, a long itinerary of locations, and engrossing uses of art and art history. The individual poems reveal her mastery of description, or irony, or form of address, or her unhesitant voicing of endearments, drifting states of mind, crisp assessments, and prickly or pleasant memory. But her books are built on a classic theme: the struggle to sustain the tension of a private, inner life."—RON SLATE, *Prairie Schooner*

The Horse Fair
"Throughout this collection, Becker offers paeans to animals, lovers and family members; to the civic-minded friend who teaches her 'the artfulness of love's responsibilities'; and to the 'unlovely' basset hound, 'legless as a walrus,' that teaches her 'to pursue my life with devotion. . . .' This generous poet is never less than attentive and responsive to the world that surrounds her."—CARMELA CIURARU, *The New York Times*

All-American Girl
"These are ambitious poems, firmly grounded in culture and concerned with the everyday struggle to make sense. Here we find a speaker grieving for her sister's death, taking joy in lesbian love, and struggling with the complexities of her own Jewish heritage. . . . The task Becker has undertaken here seems to me to be the right one. How *do* various aspects of identity fuse on a personal and cultural level?"—SUSAN HUTTON, *New England Review*

"It is Becker's undefendedness that makes this collection so strong and appealing. Whether acknowledging childhood privilege . . . or admitting her part in creating her own destiny . . . Becker's direct, fluidly accessible lyric narratives move assuredly through even the most complex emotional terrain, living with the questions, letting us know that we are with a speaker we can trust."—ALISON TOWNSEND, *Women's Review of Books*

Giacometti's Dog
"In poem after poem in *Giacometti's Dog*, Robin Becker's third book, there is a courage in the piercing details that keeps the work from flinching from feeling and avoids even a trace of self-indulgence. These poems, generous in their emotional and geographical range, speak in Becker's voice about loss, guilt, erotic yearning, and the journey of the self toward the consolations of friendship, of love, of art."—GAIL MAZUR, *Ploughshares*

Backtalk
"Becker is a visual writer, often turning her pen into a paint brush and her readers into museum-goers. I am reminded of Colette who both observes and participates with equal passion. . . ."—JEAN SEGALOFF, *Off Our Backs*

Also by Robin Becker

The Black Bear Inside Me
Tiger Heron
Domain of Perfect Affection
The Horse Fair
All-American Girl
Giacometti's Dog
Backtalk
Personal Effects

MIDSUMMER COUNT

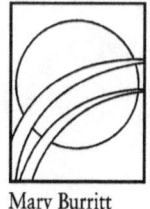

MARY BURRITT CHRISTIANSEN POETRY SERIES

Hilda Raz, Series Editor

The Mary Burritt Christiansen Poetry Series publishes two to four books a year that engage and give voice to the realities of living, working, and experiencing the West and the Border as places and as metaphors. The purpose of the series is to expand access to, and the audience for, quality poetry, both single volumes and anthologies, that can be used for general reading as well as in classrooms.

Also available in the Mary Burritt Christiansen Poetry Series:

origin story: poems by Gary Jackson
a chronology of blood: poems by Teo Shannon
A Real Man Would Have a Gun: Poems by Stacey Waite
Dream of the Bird Tattoo: Poems and Sueñitos by Juan J. Morales
Unruly Tree: Poems by Leslie Ullman
A Walk with Frank O'Hara: Poems by Susan Aizenberg
Light of Wings: Poems by Sarah Kotchian
Trials and Tribulations of Dirty Shame, Oklahoma: And Other Prose Poems by Sy Hoahwah
A Guide to Tongue Tie Surgery: Poems by Tina Carlson
Point of Entry: Poems by Katherine DiBella Seluja
Suggest Paradise: Poems by Ray Gonzalez

For additional titles in the Mary Burritt Christiansen Poetry Series, please visit unmpress.com.

MIDSUMMER COUNT

New and Selected Poems

ROBIN BECKER

UNIVERSITY OF NEW MEXICO PRESS | ALBUQUERQUE

© 2026 by Robin Becker
All rights reserved. Published 2026
Printed in the United States of America

Library of Congress Cataloging-in-Publication Data

Names: Becker, Robin, 1951– author
Title: Midsummer count : new and selected poems / Robin Becker.
Other titles: Midsummer count (Compilation) | Mary Burritt Christiansen poetry series
Description: Albuquerque : University of New Mexico Press, [2026] | Series: Mary Burritt Christiansen poetry series
Identifiers: LCCN 2025035002 | ISBN 9780826369338 paperback | ISBN 9780826369345 epub
Subjects: LCSH: American poetry—20th century | American poetry—21st century | Poetry | LCGFT: Poetry
Classification: LCC PS3552.E257 M53 2026 | DDC 811.54—dc23/eng/20250804
LC record available at https://lccn.loc.gov/2025035002

Cover illustration: *October Outside,* Charles Burchfield
Designed by Felicia Cedillos
Composed in Adobe Garamond Pro

CONTENTS

New Poems

Eating Greenland	3
First COVID-19 Summer	4
Cabin, Long Island Sound, 2020	6
Thirst	7
Fox on the Mowing	8
Harvey Is Building His Casket	10
The Well	12
The Sleeper	14
The Hardiness Zone	17
Keds	18
In Compassion's Arms	19
Affairs in Order	21
UPS	22
Fortune's Spindle	24
You Have to Stay Ahead	27
Late Apology	29
Everyone Dies	31
At the Spoon-Carving Workshop	33
The Walking Cure	35
Woman in a Landscape	37
Treif, the Wooden Pig	39
Had There Been a Woman	40
Painting Birds	42
The Pencil Poem	44
The Unfinished Painting	46

The Black Bear Inside Me

Clearing	51
Elegy for the Science Teacher	52
Bluefish, 1970	54
Scottish Melodies	55
Hearing the News	57
The Black Bear Inside Me	60
Theory	63
The Collection of the Canter	64
Security Clearance	66
The Wages of Sin	68
Men as Friends	69
Semblance	70
The Barcelona Inside Me	71
Rodeo Ben	73
Make It Plain	75
The Fix	77

Tiger Heron

Prairie Dogs	81
To a Poet	82
Hospice	84
A Last Go	86
Post Time	87
Late June Owl	88
Old Florida	90
And So Forth	92
Rescue Parable	93
Her Lies	94
Understory	95
Xenia	97
Wearing Mother's High School Ring	98

The Sounds of Yiddish	102
Divers	104
The Civil War Comes to Town	105
The Dog I Didn't Want	107
Dyke	108
When You Look at the Spines of Your Books	110

Domain of Perfect Affection

The New Egypt	115
Midsummer Count	116
Man of the Year	117
Against Pleasure	120
A Pasture of My Palm	121
Salon	122
Borderline	124
The Miniaturists	126
Summer's Tale	128
Island of Daily Life	129
Head of an Angel	131
Late Butch-Femme	132
Ok, Tucker	133
On Friendship	134
With Two Camels and One Donkey	136

The Horse Fair

The Horse Fair	141
Life Forms	148
The Wood Lot	150
Phaeton	152
The Donor	153
Raccoon	156
Wants	158

Elegy for a Secular Man	160
In Praise of the Basset Hound	165
Late Words for My Sister	166
In the Days of Awe	168
Sisters in Perpetual Motion	174
Sad Sestina	176
Adult Child	178
Against Silence	179
Why We Fear the Amish	180
The Monarchs of Parque Tranquilidad	182
Angels of the Lower East Side	184

All-American Girl

Shopping	189
The Crypto-Jews	191
My Grandmother's Crystal Ball	192
A History of Sexual Preference	193
Solar	195
Port-Au-Prince, 1960	197
Quaker Meeting, the Sixties	199
Haircut on Via Di Mezzo	201
Family Romance	203
Peter Pan in North America	205
Too Jewish	207
Contradancing in Nelson, NH	208
Midnight Swim	211
Dreaming at the Rexall Drug	212
Meeting the Gaze of the Great Horned Owl	214
Yom Kippur, Taos, New Mexico	216
Death of the Owl	218
The Roast Chicken	220

Giacometti's Dog

The Problem of Magnification	225
Living in the Barn	226
The Lover of Fruit Trees	227
Philadelphia, 1955	229
The Return	231
The Children's Concert	232
Riding Lesson	234
Giacometti's Dog	236
Conversations in July	238
Fable	240
The Bath	241
Birch Trees	242
The Subject of Our Lives	243

Backtalk

A Long Distance	247
A Good Education	248
On Not Being Able to Imagine the Future	250
Old Women and Hills	251
Sideshow	252
Prairie	254
Hockey Season	256
Captivities	258
The Conversion of the Jews	261
Morning Poem	263

Personal Effects

November	267
A Woman Leaving a Woman	268

For Bubbe Growing Older	270
The Landing	271
The Seizure	276
Bubbe 1975	277
Acknowledgments	279
Notes	281
About the Author	283

NEW POEMS
2018–2025

Eating Greenland

This year Nina chose, for her birthday's theme,
climate change. Dressed as a sperm whale,

one guest explained the melting ice sheet;
a costumed glacier reported on

the average eleven-degree rise in winter
temperatures. Nina's sister brought

a birthday cake in the shape of Greenland,
the icy, snow-covered, central region

coated with whirled coconut shavings.
Immortal Jellyfish plunged a knife

into the cake, like a Cold War scientist
extracting a core of ancient ice for Camp

Century. Secret subsurface trenches hid
a nuclear reactor and dorms for soldiers

building missile sites. Should Russia strike.
In 1965, they abandoned the lab and its toxic

waste, beneath collapsing walls of melt. This year
we ate Greenland, piece after sparkling piece.

First COVID-19 Summer

Some of us are lucky. We can swim
in a lake. We can walk on a dirt road.

Some of us live on the ninth floor where air
recirculates and the city below

pounds on. In the heat. Some of us do not
leave our apartments. Sometimes, friends shop

for us or we go to the crowded store
anyway. Anyway, a person has

to eat. Some of us live alone and have
no money to shop anyway. Some of us

work in Pick-Up and Delivery for
the grocery. For auto parts. Some

of us work checkout in Walmart, where some
men don't wear masks. Some of us are still

essential, though we don't feel essential:
look at our hours, our paychecks, our kids.

Some of us are still delivering babies in Philadelphia.
Some of us are driving across the country

in rented campers with three kids and a dog
because we think the summer is our chance

to move before the world shuts down again.

Cabin, Long Island Sound, 2020

Connecticut is a long
aquamarine word, a slim

unspooling horizon line.
I'm flush with the sublime view—

rough inlet mapped by whitecaps,
lush cloudscape galloping past

this cottage, ringed with honey-
suckle vines that sugar the air

and sweeten the path through
serviceberry, chokecherry.

This poor year of illness—
quiet rooms, closed windows—

swells and empties with the wind
that rushes through the blue screen door.

Thirst

I thought I was finished with beauty,
having shed—given away, or sold—so much
and committed myself

to necessary objects only. Ready,
I thought, for the journey to simplicity,
to matters of the soul.

But when I saw a tiny reproduction
of Eleanor Ray's *Snowy Owl, 2020*,
(6 ½ × 8 inches, oil on panel)

I had to have it—bone, eyes, turbulence,
appetite—little bird,
little hunger on the dune.

Fox on the Mowing

On the mowing's rough contours of granite and lichen
the fox caught my scent. Behind his diamond-shaped
head trailed a long, scarlet body and white-tipped tail,
evolved to light the way for kits returning to the den.

In Werner Hertzog's film, a slim fox comes to the doomed
Tim Treadwell's hand. Stroking the fox, he speaks
to the camera, his back to the bears and the misbegotten
calamity about to happen in the Alaskan woods.

The woods on either side of Harvey's field enfold the dark
and hold the cries we hear each night as fox and owl
reclaim the place. Coyotes bark. In moonlight the screams
quicken the dog who sets his snout on the window frame.

I've read that a bright carpet of reflective cells
behind the retina brings light into his eyes, improving
vision in driving rain, at dusk. Films show the fox
airborne six feet, diving into a snowbank for a mouse.

Once you've seen him, you can't *not* see him—
in the dog, for example, leaping to snatch a frisbee
from the air or wrapping his tail around his frame,
coiled tight to conserve his body heat.

The mowing, web of interdependencies, shelters
housecat and lynx, woman and bear. If you feel
you're being watched, look at the scat at your feet for a clue
to who found a meal in the field and ran to the den

to consume it, before moonlight turned the field
into a palimpsest of vulnerability—
each exposed creature legible to the lone wolf
down from Canada and the apex predator with a gun.

Harvey Is Building His Casket

on two sawhorses in the busy nave
of the barn, and when I arrive to stash
my bike, he's standing beside the box,

one hand resting on a long board. *Biodegradable*,
he says. *For a green burial, untreated white pine
is the simplest, and these common nails—they'll rust*

and disintegrate pretty quickly. It's almost done.
Pointing, he says, *That's the lid.* I look around
at the bay of electrical supplies and machine parts,

dark coils of flexible pipe and retired chairs.
Harvey likes to have a project, especially
one that will save time and money

when his family may not be thinking clearly.
*There was a guy in Alstead who used to charge
$300.00 for a box like this. Don't know if he's still at it.*

Harvey excels at thinking clearly: applying
codes and regs for electricity and plumbing,
generating goodwill at the contentious beach

by spending a morning putting in a new dock
though it's Pete-the-bully's job.
The nesting wood thrush flies at the open barn doors

as if she, too, wants to examine Harvey's casket.
I ask where it will go and he says *somewhere
on the mowing*. And, when he smiles,

I understand how he acquired four wives.
*Well, I won't be around, so that'll be someone
else's decision.* He pauses and looks at me.

Because I love him and fear that talking
about death might draw it near; because
I long for the confidence that makes

death talk possible, I don't ask how he felt
constructing the box. I point to the hayloft
and say, *I hope you store it up there for a dozen years.*

He pulls his suspenders, chuckling, *Me too*,
and already I'm regretting the locked box
inside me and these precious, wasted minutes.

The Well

This morning, in the Harrisville cemetery,
calm settles over stones and hills

where I walk in the old shade of white oaks
and sycamores with the young dog.

Beneath the peaceful surface, I sense
an undercurrent of fear—

of my government and my president,
of his State Department and his Joint Chiefs—

and beneath that, an underlying current
of sadness—for Judith and her bad diagnosis.

And beneath that sadness, the underlying
condition of gladness: as when the timid

dog finds his courage and jumps into Harrisville
Pond to retrieve a stick. And beneath that,

fury at the hatefulness aimed at protesters,
and fury at those who call the truth *fake news*.

Beneath the rage, an underlying
pleasure in the scent

of roasting fennel and tomatoes
simmering in the oven and pleasure

in cooking for my best friend and her son
and his new wife who will take pleasure

in walking uphill to my place for dinner.
Beneath these pleasures, the underlying

condition of loneliness shows up,
old colleague whose company I never

enjoyed but, with whom, nevertheless,
I shared an office. And beneath loneliness

the terror of uncertainty—
the not-knowing-what-will-come terror

that abides at the bottom of the well,
sloshing around when we drop the bucket

to pull up an underlying
gratitude for fresh, cold water.

The Sleeper

The new science will kiss you awake,
sleeping sister, with a tablet under the tongue

to stop your brain's electrical plunge—
updated version of the story I tell myself today.

Fifty years ago you slept
blanketed beneath anticonvulsants.

The doctors said you would outgrow
the seizures, but they drugged you

out of your life. You slept them off
in your pink room, eyelids fluttering

before you conked out. I wore your terror
like a mirrored shirt. You wore the little

sister's longing for my good opinion.
Mine, I shouted into the pantry, *Give her back*

to me, but you already belonged to Dilantin
and Mebaral and to our mother who took you

downtown, where the neurology tech hooked
you up for your EEG. At home you slept.

I remember how you would stop
speaking and turn away—

your child's mouth open, eyes flat.
Come back. I knew not to touch you,

but in my big-sister brain I imagined
a magic carpet on which you could float

protected, while I waited for you:
my baby sister stranded; and I, helpless.

For years, I studied your face for a clue
to the place you went. I knew not

to ask what you saw there.
They used to think a devil lived

inside San Severino's fifteenth-century woman
and in Raphael's painting of the boy

who looks up to Jesus in *The Transformation*
as the evil spirits fly from his mouth.

At six I stood on a chair
to read the prescribing information

in the bag with the pills that took
you away from me. Sometimes

they could barely rouse you. In winter,
your snowsuit and socks and boots

dried by the radiator while you slept
on the sofa, and I went out to play

in the snowstorm. To learn to take
a snowball to my neck and hurl one

into another kid's head. To hit and
get hit in return. To turn hard

like the tough boys taking aim
on the ice, their lips and fingers blue.

The Hardiness Zone

When I heard my mother weeping
in her room, I climbed from bed and stood
by hers. I felt the dread before she said
your sister, meaning the *absence seizures*
that took her, tiny seedling, away from me,
to the brain-machine lab, where wires in her scalp
recorded my sister's errant brain waves.

I held my mother's hands. She cried
until she heard my father's car and said, *Go back
to bed. I don't want him to see us here.*
My mother's fear and lonesomeness took root,
but I learned to cut the tender slips,
go dormant, toughen up, become frost-hardy, fit.

Keds

My mother believed in quality shoes
made on proper lasts of long-wearing
materials, sewn not glued. With H. Cantor,
co-owner of Sobel & Cantor, Philadelphia's
high-end store, she had this in common.

In 1955, he knelt to fit the metal Brannock's
right and left heel cups to our small feet.
Who knew Harold had organized a union?
Served as president of retail workers, Local 114?
We knew he favored stiff oxfords. He shook

his head when I pointed to the All-Star,
red, high tops. Instead, I got the girls' Keds,
a summer concession to the school-year
saddle shoes. My mother liked the men
at Sobel & Cantor's who wore bow ties and

spoke softly, carrying towers of shoeboxes,
like librarians bringing books from the stacks
with a sweet predictability. At home, my father cast
off shirt and shoes. When he screamed, mother
gripped the banister. Anything could set him off

in the booby-trapped house, where I might
plunge through a chair with loosened bolts,
pick up my humiliation with my limbs
and later, ambushed, get soaked when
a pail of water drops from my bedroom door.

In Compassion's Arms

Unjust the hierarchies
of that house in the blue world—
troubled sister cycling out
of control, cruel Father-tyrant.
Mother, I turned to the blue
world with its strangers, I turned,
forgive me, to take my chance
on arcing shoots turning spring
around trouble, as is the way of the world.
I came to Compassion's house
ringed with florets on thin stems
where Empathy lives, and
Compassion took me
into her arms, for it is in her
to circle March and April and
May with rain and kindness.
Empathy invited my sister's
ghost inside, and there
in the blue world turning
the nature of things,
I saw my unfinished sisterhood
in my turning away from her
and in my turning from forgiveness
and patience,
to assign blame.
In Compassion's arms
I saw how we made our escapes

each with her Hydra-headed troubles,
now stars of the serpent
constellation—illness, despair, suicide—
tracing my sister's story
which had always been mine.

Affairs in Order

The paperwork of course, not to mention
my lair of sweaters and shoes and properly
filed old love affairs; who will categorize
my pledges and flights? Moreover, who will care?

Ledges of books and snares, the mean quip
I can't retract, the bad choice to move or worse
to stay. Sort my options or export them to my heir?

The Life-Changing Magic of Tidying Up can't archive
the den's despairs or the attic's regrets.
Today from the menu of durable powers

I choose a trustee for death's venue. So much
to do in the wacky hours that shrink and stretch—
the late, cartoon decades of joint replacement
to fight decline, refute diminishing time.

UPS

Because it's too late for a long marriage,
I'm considering a short one
to the UPS driver in brown shorts
with a pencil parked behind her ear.
I know she likes me by the way
she takes a granola bar from my hand,
shouting "hey, thanks," as she runs
to the brown box of her truck.
I think she'd like to have coffee, talk
about her childhood, her favorite books
and movies, her vacation in P-town.
But with the requirement to stay
on schedule, make only right turns,
check oil levels and tire
pressure, she's postponed her love life.
She needs a lot of space
to come and go so I don't
try to stop her when she flies into
the driver's seat. In fact, I've parked my car
for both of us to make quick getaways.
I think we'd be a good match, with her
excellent customer relations skills,
and my respect for her ability
to lift seventy pounds unassisted.
Even a short marriage presents
certain challenges. My friend Harry says
a good marriage means one person is sleeping

in a room that's too hot, while the other
sleeps in a room that's too cold. Blind spots
may plague her, but she decorates
our traveling bedroom with string lights,
her center of gravity safely over her feet
when she leaps from a crate.
For this late-life adventure,
I'll wear my best flannel pajamas,
while my young lover, naked,
tosses blankets from her humming engine.

Fortune's Spindle

I take a hoe
to the carpet clusters
of *Fortune's Spindle*

starting to climb
the Norway Maple
Opportunistic

aerial roots
and tendrils
cling to bark

and wrap the limbs
suffocating
the host

How everything
alive wants
to stay

alive—bone
spurs growing
in the arthritic

shoulder joint—
the body's attempt
at repair

when cartilage
wears away
I'm talking

with a friend
about the indifference
of cells replicating

their codes
and the factors
that lead to mutations

We have compassion
for the body's efforts
to restore itself

after the immunotherapies
after the surgeon removes
a diseased lobe

and we praise
the three-spined stickleback
that defies

the warming oceans
by adapting to freshwater
as everything

alive wants to stay
alive even compromised
altered modified alive

You Have to Stay Ahead

of the pain, she said, it's a high speed
train gaining momentum,
headed for the town with your name.
You have to stay calm, seated, sedated
as the locomotive nears, curves
into view, freighted with your fears
of complication, infection,
pain's hue and viscosity.
You have to curry favor
with your minders, so your campaign
for more meds moves the hour
ahead. Still, you can't game
some pains—this loss, that death—
when breath moves on cold rails
to the coil car of your heart. You can't start
ahead of grief, only hold
on as it heaves you
like a pebble down the tracks.
Passenger, prepare
to disembark in pain's precinct,
because you failed
to stay ahead of it and let it
accelerate past you. Next time
(and here it comes, again)
you'll recognize relief as the thief

of sense and plan in advance—
lashed to the nonsense of *no pain
no gain*, insensible now,
unable to stay ahead
of the coming train.

Late Apology

For betraying the potential depth
of character you saw in me, I apologize.
I apologize for skimming the surface,
for *failing my pain*. For having another
woman in the wings. For hurting you.
For my febrile apologies, I apologize.
For the dinner parties I ruined
with my obsequious charm;
for currying favor; for years of flattery,
I am sorry I became someone
whose story you couldn't trust, my fabulist
renditions more fiction than fact.
I apologize for making a scene
thirty years ago at The Outdoor Store,
for not getting a grip, for my unexamined
angers. I apologize for choosing anger
instead of grief, for choosing rage
instead of laboring towards forgiveness
which was always what you wanted for me.
I apologize for not pushing myself
harder, for not getting winded. Not sticking
to the diet. I apologize for calling
the plumber before trying to fix the faucet
myself, for expensive hours on eBay, for
not being more like you, whom I admire
for your devotions to what's difficult.
I apologize for not giving you your due

when you tried to see the other point of view.
I apologize for my mean-spirited
imitations of my former colleagues,
for my gift for seeing the worst in people.
I'm sorry I didn't thank you for asking
more of me, thank you for staying
up late for our famous arguments, after which
each of us carried our burden of sadness—
you going up the meadow, me going down.

Everyone Dies

To become friendly with death
yoga practitioners repeat
"Everyone dies" once every hour.
Why are you telling me? the dog asks.
*I'm only four. I don't feel friendly
on this subject.* He curls into bed.

I practice saying "everyone dies," but
keep forgetting—and days go by
without my remembering
that everyone dies. Dog looks up.
*Didn't the yoga teacher tell you to
assume the Corpse Pose? That's depressing.*

"You have no boundaries," I tell the dog
who's wrapped his tail around his ears,
silky as satin lining my sister's casket.
Graveside, I studied the plot reserved for me,
next to great-grandmother Riva for whom
I'm named. Death and naming go together

as hands go to the heart to acknowledge
life as blessed, except for atheist Maxine who
wasn't having any of it. "Everything dies," I say
to the marsh ferns and sugar maples and
barred owl and coyote, whose kill screams
in the summer dark. With my quiet mind

somewhere I can't quite place, I see
that becoming friendly with death
will take some time, like relaxing
every hair on my head. Later, I practice
saying "everyone dies" aloud when
the dog stirs. *Did you say something to me?*

"I'm trying to accept impermanence,"
I say, "to embrace nonattachment."
That's a hard one, dog says, offering a kind look.
I forget the mantra, though I hear a song
cycle playing in the background—
change, suffering, flux, death, flow.

At the Spoon-Carving Workshop

we bowed over double-bladed knives
    to initiate the bowl, as the teacher
        instructed. Beginners, in silence,

we made tiny cuts. Tch, tch, tch, thin whorls
    rose and settled in our hair, on aprons,
        as the tall woman walked

the semicircle, taking our hands in hers,
    showing one how to angle the blade,
        repairing a gouge, explaining that grain

will reverse, suddenly, invisibly,
    and then the carver has to feel her way
        into the wood, as a hiker,

gone off trail, feels her way home.
    Then, she told this story: *Up from a nineteenth-century*
        sailing wreck, came lengths of five-hundred

year-old English maple, from which a carving
    friend made her a special gift.
        Here, she said, and pulled from a bag twenty

spoons she'd carved from the preserved maple.
    All day we found and lost the grain, all day
        the shallow bowls emerged. And then

she handed each of us a straight-blade knife
    to shape the back and neck
        and handle, showing how the thumb

controls depth, cautioning us
    not to hurry but to savor
        the motions. Then, the rough

sandpaper for an hour; then the fine
    sandpaper, grit filling the air;
        then the scrutiny, before she declared

a spoon ready for the homemade olive oil
    and beeswax rub that came in tiny tubs
        she handed out. Finished,

we lingered in the studio, admiring
    her lilac and pear dippers, extending the quiet
        hours, our hand-forged day.

The Walking Cure

My dead sister is walking the island
beaches, from Forest Beach to Driessen
and the length of the island twice.

On June 24, 1986, she walked twenty-three
and-a-half miles, noting, "Hot. 97 degrees."
On July 5, twenty miles in the rain.

Twenty-eight miles on July 7, when calories
burned totaled 2,280. On July 22, she walked
thirty miles to reach her goal: 5 pounds.

The intake papers from Duke Medical
Center show that my sister, at 114 pounds,
was below the ideal weight of 116 pounds

for medium-frame women,
as calculated by Metropolitan Life
Actuarial Tables. They admitted her anyway.

I study her food diary: 3 ounces halibut,
105 calories, 5 spears asparagus, 25 calories.
This patient has achieved remarkable success, wrote the doctor,

in his discharge letter, *bringing her weight to 105.7*.
Sometimes, we're seven and nine again,
playing Chinese checkers on the dented,

red, tin board, and she's winning because
she always did, clever despite her seizures.
She wears the tartan kilt she loved, with its silver

pin and leather buckle, knee socks and penny loafers.
Sometimes she's thirty-three with an excellent
memory—and all her life behind her. I walk,

a disconsolate a woman with unstable knees
who abandoned her sister thirty-six years ago,
who outwalked neither the phone call nor the grief.

Woman in a Landscape

I didn't need the painting to remember
the Westfield River coiling below
steep walls, the sun burning my upturned
face clear of features, my awkward arm
and bent leg trying to appear relaxed
on the rock for Deborah practicing
her figure painting. Naked, I wanted
to be useful to her in the color fields
of July and August—where I ached
to shed my shame with my clothes,
to trade my barely acceptable
twenty-four-year-old body for one
I could admire as I admired hers.
Still, when she sent me a PDF of the fifty-
year-old painting—dark hemlocks and pines
hemming the water—I remembered walking
downhill with my flashlight, a dumb city
girl spooked on dirt roads by weird sounds.
I tried to be brave, each day at my desk,
tried to find language for my lesbian desire
on drives up light-drenched Route 9
with Deb through Hadley and Williamsburg.
When I look at the painting now
I wish I had found some tenderness
then for the person lying on the rock—
ardent, earnest with her imperfect
young breasts and belly.

I wish I'd found her comely against
the silver-blue river, rising with her
doubts and fears on reliable legs
all summer to leap from rock to shore.

Treif, the Wooden Pig

Size of a weathervane, she hung it
over the desk where she wrote and ate.
Walnut folk art, the warm round
shape conveyed farm life and death
in the starkest wooden terms.
As carved barnyard pig in the toybox,
it showed an affectionate nature
befriending the doomed calf.
As butcher's sign and market roast,
the pig returned her hungry gaze
with acceptance, wiser than her appetite.
Once it spoke to her
asking to be held and stroked.
Oh, meat forbidden by Kosher law!
No French pork *crépinette*
no medallions glazed
with peaches.
She stood on a chair,
caressed its smooth finish,
humming a Bach Prelude
which taboo pig quite enjoyed.

Had There Been a Woman

for Sally Greenberg

Had I heard a woman's voice
chanting the sacred
Dayenu

Had there been a woman
at the bimah wearing a tallit
Dayenu

Had she carried the Torah
up and down the center aisle
of the synagogue
Dayenu
as women and men leaned in touching
the silken cover

Had she an office where I could confide
my fears my shame
Dayenu
seek her counsel in safety

How many of us might have
felt worthy
Dayenu

had a woman scholar rabbi celebrant
welcomed us into the texts
as vital and necessary

interpreters of law and narrative
Dayenu
How can we but honor those
who persisted

without encouragement but with faith
in themselves
Dayenu
and in a Judaism

of deliberative compassionate
women's minds
Dayenu

Had there been a woman rabbi
at the hospital at the gravesite
Dayenu
we might have taken a seat
at the head of the Seder table

where today Sally says the kiddush
washes her hands blesses the parsley
dipping it into the tears
Dayenu
of our enslavement

Painting Birds

for Rabbi Marcia Plumb

The cardinal jerks his mask and crest.
I ask my brush to match his twitch,

stout beak and birdy snood, a word
the first-century rabbis might have used,

who had ten words for joy, including *rina*
for singing and *pitzcha* for bursting

into song, like the wood thrush I heard
all summer long but never saw.

They had the word *sasson* for joy tinged
with sorrow—the Destruction of the Temple—

and for rejoicing when the swifts
returned to cracks in the Wailing Wall.

Same massive limestone blocks, same day
every year. For thousands of years.

In my painting, the swift's forked tail
feathers guide pitch and yaw, but I fail

to convey the way the birds eat
and sleep and mate on the wing.

Of the ten types of joy, I know best the one
that includes disappointment after reaching,

playing the Bach badly but playing, failing
to capture flight but trying. For this joy,

chedra, the rabbis considered human instinct—
and the need to push past Despair. Anger. Fatigue.

They say the swift can fall asleep in Jerusalem
and wake up in Jordan. Still flying.

The Pencil Poem

I should have known where this was going
when I ordered three, mint green, Craft Design
Technology pencils (for musicians)
from the store on Orchard Street and then fell
in love with the German, glass-cannister sharpener.

Who wouldn't want the Camel HB pencil
with its ferrule-less eraser, the best choice
for word scramblers? And for a mere
$11.75 I can try out six carefully curated
varieties in the Crossword Puzzle Sampler Set.

Pencils for musicians write sonatas and quartets,
erase nicely and hold their points. Magic
pencils write in three colors. With the flat
carpenter's pencil (which won't roll off
the drafting table), I design a hutch and bookcase,

while the Technograph from Switzerland renders
architectural details. For my left-handed
friends, the smudge-resistant sampler set comes
with a special, skinny eraser. Who knew
that a set of pencils for lovers of pens

would include the Palomino Blackwing 602
made in Japan from California cedar?

Oh, the bipartisan power of the baseball
scoring pencil, round barreled,
made in the USA and sold in a box of six!

The Editor's pencil with two heads—red
and charcoal—will revise your novel for $3.00.
With the Nataraj Ruby 621, made in Mumbai,
grade essays and exams, and for a neon highlight,
go with Caran d'ache Graphicolor.

Who doesn't need a nickel-plated
pencil cap? A mesh or sailcloth or leather
storage case? Or a yellow pencil box
copied from the plastic ones we used as kids?
Should the pencil go extinct, I'll go retro

on eBay, like Oletimey442 selling
Nintendo parts, linotype, and 8-track tapes.
How my pleasure center burns for the Staedtler
HB Graphite—the unquenchable craving,
unlike the object, always aflame.

The Unfinished Painting

Canvas shows through
an inference of low-slung rooftops—
the paint thin to suggest rather
than insist on frame cottages,

pond, fragile footbridge
coming into focus at dawn
after a rainstorm; receding
at dusk into a spectral village

edged in firs—and dissolving
against my will into linen weave.
I keep coming back
to the muzzy shoreline—swatch

of wet-footed grasses and rocks,
a deferred undertaking that now never
will resolve into summer or fall.
The painter who abandoned this

landscape left me its abundant
incompleteness, a paradise
of possibility so spare I can walk
the pond's perimeter and disappear

into the homespun mystery—
the moment someone called her away,
and the painter's attention shifted
forever from the emerging prospect—

all the mineral spirits escaping.

THE BLACK BEAR
INSIDE ME

Clearing

Since Harvey's on his tractor for the first
cutting of the summer I'm glad I picked
paintbrush hawkweed and daisies early
this morning   Wild turkeys squawking at the edge
of the mowing complain his noisy occupation
displeases them exposed to fox and falcon now
Where will they hide to feed   He chose today
for the dry breeze rifling rush and bluestem

All of July and August lie ahead but I want only June
light dappling mountain ash   They say to live in the present
requires we let go every second of our lives
He keeps a mowing by mowing for July's meadow rue
and asters   To live in the present they say become a fern
a prism a membrane through which time mows

Elegy for the Science Teacher

Maria D. Peters, 1915–2013

Mrs. Peters has died at ninety-eight and I'll never get a chance
to apologize for all the trouble I brought to seventh grade
science, where she demonstrated how the folding-door
spider dug ten-inch tunnels into rotting logs with
spiny mandibles and lined the walls with silk
and left a bit hanging out to form a door from which
it catapulted after dark. In the circus of natural history
I was the class clown, she the vivarium; her faith included

the decomposing log and the chemical chatter of beetles.
Born in Breslau in 1915 she spoke with a German accent
about *British Soldiers*—the red-capped lichen that thrives
on decaying conifer—and the slimy slug that propels itself
with an undulating muscular foot along the forest floor.
Colonies of carpenter ants and bees proved the Quaker
principle of cooperation: her ecosystem, her religion. In London
during the war, she taught Basque refugees by speaking Latin.

Ah, Mrs. Peters, did the inter-relatedness of fungal spore and wind
move you to drive the Schuykill Expressway every Tuesday
to pack up clothes for needy families? I could not appreciate
the watershed you made of your life, linking all living
things by a common course. Twenty years ago, at a reception
you told me of your father's best friend, a Jewish scientist who
refused to leave Germany in 1935. My father begged him to go
you said. My father cried you said. He never forgot him.

I failed to plot the simple graph on Darwinian snails.
She pioneered the PA School of Horticulture for Women
where girls kept bees, canned fruit, learned farm carpentry
and soil science, studying the energetic sow bug with seven pairs
of legs and a carapace of overlapping plates. Recently, people
have come around to her belief in conservation, sustainability.
A tiny woman, sometimes for emphasis she would pull
out the bottom drawer of her desk and stand on it. We all laughed.

Bluefish, 1970

My first summer in P-town neighbors taught me *Puttanesca*
oil capers olives marinating fish in the tiny kitchen
of the three-bay half cottage I rented with my unemployment
check blocks off Commercial Street
where the drag queens called *Hello, Dolly*
and bluefish sold for $3.99 lb all summer

At Race Point fisherman anchored in wet sand fought
the indigo wind the inky surf bluefish on their lines and
in coolers and in the A & P where I stared at the handsome
butch women with their girlfriends in town for a week
from Kansas and Ohio desire thrumming the narrow
streets and the clamorous angles of Provincetown's

rooftops desire incoming as the tide I read and wrote
by day and thereby earned my nightly trip to the women's bar
to disco to cigarettes and the compulsive disappointment of leaving
alone at 2 a.m. for home past revelers sharing pizza at *Spiritus*
you never know what the senses will retain just last week
at the market I overheard *look they have bluefish today*

Scottish Melodies

When they play the strathspey
Marshall wrote for Mrs. Gordon of Park,
the fiddler remembers the mowing
meadow once on common land,
and when they play "Marquis of Huntley's Farewell"
the pianist knows the son must leave his home,

and the open field system
must give way to enclosure and lament.
To the "Mortlach Reel" and
"Anderson's Rant" we will dance
in the hills of displacement
and in the town hall of good manners

where the youngest learns to keep
her weight on the outside foot
and circle right. Of the history
of northeast Scotland, we have 262 tunes
that may be played at different speeds
whether for dancing or listening

to the tragedy of the commons,
in matters of resources like air and water
which must be taught to every generation—
like learning to spot by keeping your eyes
on your partner's eyes when dancing,
so as not to get dizzy and spin

down the middle without your feet.
To the tunes of William Marshall,
played in Nelson, New Hampshire, the caller
will ask all dancers to bow to their neighbors,
a practice the Highlanders carried with them
from the Clearances to Cape Breton and Cape Fear.

Hearing the News

In memory of Maxine Kumin

I call the dog and walk
    down the mowing
        wondering how dying

dares to haunt
    this breezy summer day.
        An old question

you'd reply and mention
    Auden, his way
        with boys falling from skies.

You'd hoist a hay bale
    with one strong arm—wisps sailed
        among the flies—

then plunge your scoop
    into the bin. Loose grain
        clattered like rain.

I loved to watch you move
    around the barn.
        Tan, in a sleeveless shirt,

you cinched the girth
    on a bay horse. The farm
        bustled with guests

who wanted to be close
    and you played host
        to all. How blessed

to follow you
    uphill and skinny dip
        where stocked trout flipped . . .

Summer ripened the new
    pole beans and peas.
        From trees marked for thinning

wafted spinning
    red ribbons. Did it ease
        your agnostic

perspective (Jewish soul?)
    to see bodies of whole
        beloved horses lifted

into graves you pondered
    from your windows?
        I move with

heavy wonder
    at your slowing. You'd groan
        snap out of it,

then go upstairs to pick
on your poems,
your *bone pile*.

The Black Bear Inside Me

All summer I elude them—
who think they want to see

my three cubs someone
said she spotted

on the gravel road that severs
thick woods

near a row of mailboxes,
by the stream;

who take the path down
and up the mowing

with baskets on their arms,
fearful

when they hear me
huff or blow.

They know
I will outrun, outswim,

out-climb, bluff-charge,
and in winter

drop my heart rate
from forty to eight beats a minute

in my den of
wind-thrown trees.

They know they will take
me in the September

kill, harvesting
my kind with dogs

and guns, and they know
we haven't taken one of them

since 1784 in this state
where five thousand black bears

clear carcasses
of deer and moose

and sow
fruit trees and shrubs.

They know they need us
who are so like them

our numbers tell
the story, yes, the land

that supports us
supports them; without us,

adapted to scarcity and woodland
loss, they're going down.

Theory

As the animal returns on a beaten path
to the den, we go back over the facts
certain we ignored clear signs.

I left for Italy that summer, though
she had quit her job and moved back home.
I knew it signaled a bad turn but chose

the Tuscan love affair in the seventeenth-century
olive mill. We say we *survive* our siblings'
suicides, meaning we stood with our parents

at the unthinkable graves. In one theory,
the troubled family sacrifices one member,
as plants surrender leaves in times of drought.

The Collection of the Canter

Three days a week, into that stable of pre-adolescence
I strode, where the smell of *Absorbine*
and hoof dressing rose astringent from the cross ties,
where a girl in muddy boots circled a curry comb,
where the language of bridles and bits rolled in my mouth
as I said *D-Ring Snaffle* and *Rubber Pelham*,
Kimberwicke and *Hackamore*. And I learned

a horse must come to the bit, you cannot force
him to collect himself, you must ask him
with your weight and legs and hands. The girl
walked her horse into his stall, unbuckled the halter,
and hugged the V where the breastplate left
a sweaty place she scrubbed away.

We grazed them on braided nylon ropes or leather
lead shanks. Tornado, the open jumper, wore quilted leg wraps
daredevil Debbie knelt to secure. Summer
Saturdays we trailered to shows, entered *classes*
where I came to understand *class* as *the father who rises
at five to pack hoof pick and shedding blade*. My father
didn't see the point, came late, wore white loafers. I was

the only Jew until Judy Cohen came with her black
thoroughbred, her father, the rabbi, known to my family.
Throatlatch, cavesson, browband, laced rein. I loved
the bridle's vocabulary, the music of *martingale* and *curb chain*

hanging in the tack room, where I came to understand *class*
as Stubben saddles with brass name plates. I never

had the confidence but I had an ear. I never liked
the nervous circling before the jumps or jumping
but I loved the words *oxer, wing standards, jump cup,*
women in show coats and proper fawn breeches, gloved hands
steady at the withers, at the sitting trot, at the collected
canter, over the jumps and then the slow circle to mark
a faultless round, applause, doff of the hat.

She swung her leg over and casually slid off,
reins in one hand, a Coke someone gave her in the other,
glamorous even in the exercise paddock, counting off strides
between jumps. You never lose your early memory of class: tack room
with gleaming bridles hanging in a figure-8 style, where
you waited, belonging, with the others for your ride home.

Security Clearance

The tall one wore a grey raincoat, and the
short one in a beige raincoat said they knew
he'd been my student, they wouldn't take much
of my time, it was a government matter.
They sat in the chairs where my students sit
for conferences and took out notebooks,
like students, and then one asked, *Does he have
any reason to do harm to America?*
Once Daniel brought to seminar a poem
about Mount Namsan and the Han River,
set in Korea, where he'd gone over
Christmas break to see his mother, a lieutenant
stationed in Yongsan. I urged him to think
about grad school but he wanted Army Intelligence.
What did he like to do in his spare time?
He wrote poetry, I said. *He wrote poetry*, the
short one repeated and the tall one wrote it down,
repeating *poetry*. *How would you characterize
his temperament? Mild?* one coached.
Easily riled? The smart girl with spiky,
purple hair liked to sit beside him. The only
black student in the class, he never spoke
about race when race surfaced in seminar.
Use of drugs or alcohol? I called on him
when we talked about craft. *Daniel*, I asked,
what do you hear in the music of these lines?
He studied all weekend, an Honors student,
a double-major. He often put his head down

on the desk, resting as the others drifted in,
as if he needed to conserve energy.
On the incarceration of black men
in our country, on the presidency
of Barack Obama, we never spoke. *Would he
have any reason to be angry
at the United States?* We looked at his line
turns, talked about syntax and diction. He read
Keats and Komunyakaa; loved choosing
odd verbs and offbeat images; knew indirection
sometimes works best—shifting pace and tone.
*What can you say that would help us evaluate
Daniel's suitability for sensitive work?*
The last time I saw him, he said he'd gotten
some sleep and was moving to DC
to await his security clearance.
You could get a fellowship to grad school,
I repeated. *You wouldn't have to pay.*
You always pay, he said and shook my hand.
Thank you for your time, the tall one said.
*Is there anything you would like to add
about Daniel's character or work ethic?*
Once he brought to class a poem in which
the speaker takes a gun apart and reassembles
it after cleaning. I figured his mother
taught him how to do it: the poem
showed a loving attention to detail.

The Wages of Sin

New neighbors down the road posted a sign
that reads *The wages of sin is death. None
come to the Father but by me.* Atrocity

alters how language comes to us. *Orlando*:
American shorthand for tragedy
no Magic Kingdom can undo. *Newtown.*

Columbine. The semi-automatic slaughters
light names with a detonating charge.
He who worked for Disney's wages will return

neither to his father nor to anyone.
How to love my neighbor as myself, then?
I can't. Gay kids who went to dance at Pulse

pay with their lives, while down the road, the sign—
God's gift to us: eternal life through Christ—

Men as Friends

I have a few which is news to me
Tom drops by in the mornings with his travel
mug my mother would call it a coffee klatch

we review our terrible histories with fathers
and talk about the father he's become and how much
it will cost to replace gutters the ice brought down

and then there's soft-spoken Harvey
with whom I enjoy long pauses in conversation about how
they raised the Nelson town hall and put a foundation underneath

during which we both look up at Mt. Monadnock and then down
at the ground and then back at each other silence precipitating
the pretty weather we share before he goes inside for lunch

when I had to pack up my office Tom boxed
and loaded books into my car I didn't think he'd want to
but his idea of friendship includes carrying heavy things

at the dog park the retired Marine with the schnauzer
asked *Do you have a husband?* I replied *I don't care for men
in that way* as a Marine James mostly played cards

on a supply ship now he mostly hunts and fishes
climbs his orchard ladder for my Cortlands
and in trout season leaves, in my fridge, two rainbows

Semblance

The dog I love is turning into my father
an old man I have to humor to get up
do his business he even growls like my father

and gives me the eye I never know what kind
of mood I'll find when he wakes from a nap
and with stiff joints makes his way to the kitchen

when it rains he turns from the door whining
surly when it snows he refuses to wear a coat
when people visit he remembers his old

manners and sometimes joins us on the couch
and falls asleep snoring like my father who
never had much use for my conversation

and showed his teeth when I
displeased him collared as he was
and made to heel by his betters

after guests leave he stares at his food sometimes
I ignore him sometimes I plunge my hands
into the smelly stuff and he eats from my palm

The Barcelona Inside Me

Give me, again, the fairy tale grotto
with the portico-vaulting overhead.
Let me walk beneath the canted columns
of Gaudi' s rookery, spiral
along his crenelated Jerusalem
of broken tiles, crazy shields.
Yes, it's hot as hell and full
of tourists at the double helix,
but the anarchists now occupy
the food court, and the Arcadian dream
for the working class includes this shady
colonnade cut into the mountainside.
I've postponed my allegiance to
the tiny house movement, to the 450
square feet of simple, American maple
infrastructure and the roomy
mind suspended like a hammock
between joists. Serpents and castle
keeps shimmer, and a mosaic invitation
to the Confectionery gets me a free
café con leche on *La Rambla*,
where honeycombed apartments bend
on chiseled stone and host
floating, wrought-iron balconies.
I think I'll move into Gaudi's dream
of recycled mesh, walk barefoot
on his flagstone tiles

inscribed with seaweed
and sacred graffiti
from pagan tombs.
O, Barcelona of chamfered corners!
And chimneys of cowled
warriors! From Gaudi's Book
of Revelations, I invite the goblet
and the stone Mobius strip
to a tapas of grilled prawns and squid.

Rodeo Ben

1893–1985

Happy Trails to you, Bernard Lichtenstein,
Tailor to the Stars, who outfitted Gene Autry
and Roy Rodgers and little riders like me
at 6240 North Broad Street and Godfrey,
across from the Hot Shoppe,

where, in 1959, my father ordered the mouth-
numbing *orange freeze*. We watched
the door for bronco busters coming in for lunch,
and once he swore he saw Hopalong Cassidy
get into a Cadillac. Bernie, you recast the man

from Lodz—immigrant stitcher for *Blue Bell*
and *Wrangler*—as *Rodeo Ben*, the Yiddish-speaking
King of Cowboy Wear. From Cincinnati, Leonard
Franklin Slye emerged a singing buckaroo;
Lucille Wood Smith fashioned herself into

the wholesome Dale Evans, riding *Buttermilk*,
envy of young cowgirls who copied her
style at *Rodeo Ben's* in fringed vests and
turquoise shirts embroidered with cactus flowers.
I wanted tan breeches and a black

melton jacket, a velveteen-covered helmet
and tall leather boots. Ben sold those, too.
For "English" riders, out came ratcatcher and stock
pin with a tiny horse's head encased in acrylic.
"Don't Fence Me In" played in the background

as I tried to look like Althea Roger-Smith, British
show-jumper and winner of the Queen Elizabeth Cup.
My father pulled out his wallet, I gathered up my boxes,
dreaming myself into a tale of pluck,
no longer that terrified girl at the post-and-rail

who couldn't get her timing right and rose
seconds late from the saddle and who, when her horse
veered from the fence, corkscrewed headfirst into it.
I never left that frightened girl behind
in the dressing room at *Rodeo Ben's*,

though I tried. Each time I saw the ambulance
parked by the show ring, I knew it waited for me,
and for my father, climbing in beside me, fumbling
with the buttons on the expensive shirt, as the siren
rang out our sweet, unsustainable dreams.

Make It Plain

in memory of Miriam Goodman, 1939–2008

At August's end I make a last bouquet—
the asters (white and purple), goldenrod,
a nodding thistle, baneberry, hawkweed.

I use my friend's old *Field Guide*; in the book,
her twenty-year-old chart of flowers glimpsed
for two decades from June to fall's first freeze.

Dear Miriam, your handwritten life list
betrays you as a lover of the world
and of the words that make it plain to us

though documents, like directions, can confound
when someone says *turn left where the ochre
house used to sit* or *seen off Chesham Road.*

You suffered all the usual assaults,
the body's failures, friendships gone adrift.
Maybe that's why I like to think of you

pulling off the road in mid-July
to jot down *sundew, pitcher plant, toadflax,*
and *strange pink cluster near Leadmine Quarry.*

This search to match a flower to its name
can lend a certain order to the day
as well as give a shape to solitude,

yours, mine. Brave, like you, a little lonely
my bouquet on your table stands.

The Fix

Harvey says *it'll hold for now* meaning the gasket
he's rigged to stop the leak in the water tank

it's what he says when he conjures a grasp of wood
notched to catch a door that always swung shut his supply

of couplers and pipe makes visible the makeshift
nature of our daily operations the contingencies

he concocts from the hardware store of his truck to *hold
for now* electrical and structural salvations he believes

in the temporal the neighborly the seasonal the salvaging
of all reusable metal and wood in the inevitable

breakdowns coming towards us about which he chuckles
installs a stop valve and tightens the joint by hand

knowing a system undergoing a thermodynamic process
can never completely return to its previous state

and a leaky valve in faucet or heart requires mechanical
gods who say wiping their hands *it'll hold for now*

sutured duct-taped now rubber-banded now
stretching elastic now to reach at least next week

TIGER HERON

Prairie Dogs

for Khyber Oser
and in memory of Matthew Shepard (1976–1998)

They tenanted the far high-school field,
the dispossessed Lotaburger lot, the dog run.
Shifty, sometimes rabid, they dared to stand

upright, almost human, and stare. I feared their deft
hands, the shrug of shoulders before they spiraled
underground. That day one hung panting on a twist

of barbed wire; front paws scored the dirt.
A ripped haunch, roiling and bloody, flashed,
and I turned away, yanking the dog behind me,

when my young cousin whispered *what's
this*, and groped for a stick to free the leg,
and when that didn't work, he knelt in the trashy

run, his face close to the scrabbler, fingers
plying the greasy, furred gash, the entrails
glazed with flies which might have deterred

someone else, but he sat, now cross-legged,
unwinding the wrecked limb the way the hands
that lifted the boy in Wyoming must have worked.

To a Poet

for Maxine Kumin

You never found comfort in doctrine
    but in the winter
coats of your horses and in the climbing

    tendrils of your beans
all making their way into the strict lines
    to which I now return

You set the cool spring trail ride on Amanda
    alongside the slaughterer's
bullet slamming sidelong

    You set the body
swimming in the pond, mind dissolving
    and shucking off its burden

You let the woman lie down with the bear
    and migrate
with the arctic caribou Your anguish

    in aligning loss
with love became metrical protests
    as a gorgeous May

afternoon enters every window of the house
    where someone is sick
and someone is reading to the sick

    and someone makes supper using
every language available to say *nourishment,*
    mystery, wisdom

and *I will sleep on the floor in your room*

Hospice

I wanted to believe in it, the word
softer than *hospital* but still not *home*—

like any other frame house on the street,
it had a lawn, a door, a bell—

inside, our friend lay, a view
of the garden from her room but no lift

to raise her from the bed. A sword,
the sun plunged across the cotton blankets.

I wanted dying to be Mediterranean,
curated, a villa, like the Greek sanatoria

where the ancients cared for their sick
on airy porticos and verandas

with stone paths that led to libraries.
A nurse entered her room and closed the door.

For the alleviation of pain, I praise
Morpheus, god of dreams, unlocking

the medicine drawer with a simple key,
narcotic placed beneath the tongue.

In the hall, the volunteer offered us coffee.
How could I think the Mozart in G major

we played to distract her could distract her?
Or marble sculpture in the atrium?

A Last Go

My mother takes the world into her mouth,
she takes the sour-cream coffee cake and
the *rugelach* with walnuts and currants.
She wants a pecan raisin loaf, two loaves,
See's suckers, and *mandelbrodt*,
and I'll take her hunger any way I can,
mainlining my mother's desires, finding
in her appetites the young woman—
tortoise-shell sunglasses and dark hair
pulled back in a silk scarf—
who gunned the white Ford Galaxy, hardtop
convertible, a ringer for Jackie O.
This is her reward for years
of tuning deprivation
like a violin, of learning to do more on less
and less until she lived on argument, solo
performance, dry toast and black coffee, the fish
dish halved. Now that medical studies show
the skinny live longer, she's gained
the sweet taste of being right all along.
Go ahead, Ma, try the ginger scones,
the lemon poppyseed cake.
All the hours you hoarded have turned
into years; there's time for a last
go at pleasure.

Post Time

What my father loved about the track—
time compressed into three-minute segments,
the idea of someone losing his shirt
or a few bucks, or winning big . . .

He loved the last-minute window,
gamblers tense to place the last winning bet,
and all the losing tickets he stepped on
walking to the boy who ran to get his car.

Once, at ten, sleepless, I carried to his room
some nameless fear I wanted him to soothe.
He told me his secret: to lie on one side
and concentrate to keep away the dread.

I used to think only of my father's anger.
Now I think of his loneliness.

Late June Owl

    They say it's a bad
summer for ticks, a good summer
       for daylilies

(Quality Control likes
      to measure and evaluate
with continuous monitoring)

    They say my friend
has a few weeks, maybe a month
      but you never know

As the raptor people know
      how to keep the orphaned
screech owl before release

      may his keepers
open the airy nets of their patience
      when he tries them

They say the screech owl's trill
      has more than four
individual calls per second

      They say they can
barely hear his voice, more like wind
      than words

They say the owlet will leave
    the open cage when fully flighted
and capable of hunting

    They say the dying
will sometimes wait until everyone
    has left the room

Old Florida

    When the soon-to-be famous hurricane
hurried to their neighborhood, I begged them

        to leave. Rain made a cassoulet of the parking lot;
           winds juggled giant palms like rolling pins;

    shy herons took cover beneath awnings
and stood like museum guards in doorways—

        but my parents hunkered down, children
           under desks in the '50s, the storm their personal blitz.

    I cried, I screamed over the phone, but they rejected
the generator-backed shelter I found, chose canned

        goods and bunker, until the phone died—and I consigned them
           to their neighbors, their luck, their blood thinners.

    Eighty-seven years old, they hid on the ninth floor,
elevator out, infrastructure crumbling, but more

        than death or thirst they feared their daughter
           with her talk of evacuation.

    Leaving home, even for natural disaster, made them
refugees, registrants in a vast and subtly

  documented conspiracy to remove them
    from their apartment to assisted living.

  Neighbors found them sweating in their foxhole,
ferried batteries, salami, and ice,

    and when the power came back, they phoned
      to report that hardship brought out the kindness

    in people, wasn't it fortunate they stayed in their home?
And where was my faith in human goodness?

And So Forth

In the last years of his life, my father
concluded every sentence *and so forth*.
Three-syllable glaze, the phrase purveyed
the sweet aftertaste of icing, a hopeful
sufficiency. *I went to the doctor and so forth*.
I pictured him coming about, a sail
tightening to the wind in a graceful
arc, the whole boat of him forthwith gliding.
Never one for details, he'd body forth
with his spasm of sonants—*and so forth*—
shellacking particulars. No solvent
loosened names or dates,
and my mother died before she chose
laziness or cognitive loss. No matter.
Let others blather on with unnecessary hype;
my father made do with his small class
of words. Conjunctions fortified him,
lent him congress and congregation, as in
I had lunch with the boys and so forth,
to which I, blabbermouth daughter,
append a buoyancy of pastrami and coleslaw.

Rescue Parable

Though saved from starvation and given
his own name, bowl, bed;

though he wears the tags
of ownership and veterinary care;

though he sleeps in the sun with his cat
who grooms him in the autumn afternoon;

he carries every bone to the back of the yard,
digs with his forepaws a grave,

and with his nose, dutiful as one enslaved,
covers with dirt the coming poverty.

Her Lies

Carpenter bees continue to pock
the fascia boards, drill the wood
into runnels of connecting troughs.

Humming above me, they debride
the gallery, disappear inside.

They say these bees can hollow out a house
before anyone comprehends the tiny
piles of dust, almost invisible, on the floor.

Understory

for Eloise Klein Healy and Colleen Rooney

I woke to howler monkeys screaming at dawn.
The false-eyed iguana changed from orange to green.

In the raftered lobby, a teal-winged macaw
screeched *hello baby* and the Jesus

lizard ran across the infinity pool
that met the sky. The deceptive cadence

of Bach's Passacaglia and Fugue in C minor
rang in my headphones in the forest

that made its own clouds and thus continually wept.
Del Monte pineapples flanked the road to Tortuguero

where the forbidden Caribbean sparkled with sharks.
In the mangrove, a fallen log opened its mouth,

and leaves doubled in size every day
above a chevroned tiger heron wading in the slough.

I beached the kayak below tiered and pedestaled
trees festooned in droplets, trees studded with pink

epiphytes, their holdfasts strong as barbed wire.
After a brief fracas with bullet ants and poison

frogs, I revived at the thatched tiki bar
and added a gray-headed kite to my life

list beneath boa constrictor and sloth.
Seven years together, now we no longer speak.

The rainforest absorbs decay in a lyric.
Like a bird in a mist net, the half-life of betrayal.

Xenia

for Leslie Lawrence

Most days that summer your old dog came up,
in the searing heat, with a failing heart,
from your place, the half mile uphill to mine—

up the steep rise, past the pastured goats, on
the buggy trail that swerves through blueberries.

As you pointed out, *The Odyssey*
is full of tears, everyone weeping
to find and lose and find each other again.

Spent, he struggled the last two hundred yards,
ears low, chest heaving. Hearing
the jangling of his tags I knew the gods

had chosen me to praise him for his journey,
offer food and water, a place to sleep.

Wearing Mother's High School Ring

I

Her maiden name, etched in the ring, means *wine
merchant* in Yiddish, so I toast

her inaugural self—
arching and graceful as maiden grass,

a filly who hasn't won a race but carries
the gene for heart and mildness, the middle,

dutiful child of three, the peacemaker,
translating from Yiddish for little Bubbe

upstairs. When Germany fires on the Polish
army at Danzig, when Gandhi starts a hunger

strike protesting British rule, she's eighteen,
walking the Boardwalk in Atlantic City

with the man I found on Ancestry.com.

II

Because I want to think that she felt joy,
because she will marry my father

nine years after the annulment,
I choose her senior year, 1939.

This blond, Jewish, Lithuanian boy
with the great body takes her to the prom.

She wears the Olney High onyx and gold
class ring on a slender finger. He likes

to dance, so she complies. Self-consciousness
usually cripples her but not tonight,

not tonight, oh please! Let her find her voice
like Marian Anderson, denied a concert hall,

singing outside to seventy-five thousand at the Lincoln Memorial.

III

Let's leave her in Fralinger's, on the Boardwalk,
buying saltwater taffy to take home.

I take her guy aside, ask him, *What makes
her happy? What music does she like?*

*Where in the world would she like to go?
And you, Mr. X! Why do you love her?*

We've got the rest of our lives to be sad,
he says. *I'm teaching her to drive a car.*

*After the World's Fair, we'll go to the Bronx,
listen to Lou Gehrig, the luckiest man alive.*

*Listen. It's going to get bad. Jews living in
occupied Poland will transfer to ghettos.*

On the radio, Billie Holiday sings "Strange Fruit."

IV

She wakes to the headline: *U.S. Denies
Access to Jewish Refugees.* She knows

it's going to get bad. In love, she wants
a home of their own, war jobs to fund

new lives. She still believes it's possible
to dream big dreams, and I would leave her there

with that belief, twirling the high school ring,
spinning before the mirror in her room,

a tomboyish beauty with no knowledge
yet of crematoria and the Neutrality Act

Franklin Roosevelt will advocate.
The Wizard of Oz hits Philly theaters

and "Over the Rainbow" makes the charts.

The Sounds of Yiddish

splat like *matzoh* broken and dropped
in the egg-milk mix for *matzohbrei*.

They knock you deep in the *kishkes*.
They smart—*kine ahora*—with the *schtick* of the canny

mensch who knows *schlock* when she sees it.
You think I'm a *pischer*? Don't *drey mir kop*.

Yiddish knows an example is not proof,
gives a *tumler* with a *pisk* the barbed shrug.

When a schlimazel sells an umbrella the sun comes out.
You should grow like an onion with your head

in the ground. Yiddish hisses with chicken *schmaltz*
sizzling for *knishes*. Not invited to the luncheon?

Don't worry; her *knaidlach* don't float.
Like the Sami with many words for snow,

we have many for fool. *Shtunk. Schlepper. Schlemiel.*
Shmuck. Hear that rumbling across Ukraine?

Yiddish ran from a posse of hazards when
my Bubbe left her *shtetl*, Russians at her back

and a mongrel, Middle High German in her mouth.
A language is a dialect with an army and a navy

the saying goes. To which my peasant relatives reply,
Spare us what we can learn to endure.

Divers

Dominican Republic

In our gear we circled the dying reef—
gray pillar and star, algal blooms choking
embroidered brain coral come to grief

and rubble. Purple sea fans blew beneath
domed colonies, silken nets floating.
In our gear we circled the sickened reef

depleted by carbon sink and bleached
by rising temperatures. We spoke in
sign, pointed shriveled fingers to griefs

incised, grooved, silted over. Angels leached
from caverns; we followed remote in-
lets where a brittle darkness shingling the reef

housed a school of blue tang that breached
the gloom. A pair of ocean sturgeon smote
my mask in the doomed, ultraviolet light of grief

that lit wrasse, spotted damselfish, and sweep.
When a goatfish jackknifed from the slope
I shuddered with hope for the sessile reef—
and surfaced with my human griefs.

The Civil War Comes to Town

What could I say to the 128th Pennsylvania
Infantry Regiment reenactor,
pouring coffee by the Company C fire
with his sons? *Have some bacon*, he offered,
gesturing to the iron pot, blackened
by the 1863 campaigns—Chancellorsville
and Wapping Heights, Auburn Mills and Kelly's Ford.

We followed behind after father, one
costumed boy offered. Then he ran off
with his wooden rifle to shoot his brother.
My dog lay down in the sun. *Now we've got
a Company mutt*, one blue-suited soldier said.
I stood by the chess board, watching the soldiers
mull over their moves. *We mustered in August

of 1862*, my reenactor told me. *Coffee?*
They offered me a seat at the writing table
where a recruit struggled with a letter
to Po River, Virginia, May 10, 1864.
Inside the tent, someone hemmed a coat,
pulling the needle through coarse, blue wool.
Young men rubbed Huberd's Shoe Grease on brogans,

and soon I fell to mending blankets.
I stuffed my hair into a cap and took
the role of Rob, cross-dressing scout who saved
three hundred souls. Thus, I joined the men
of Company C; we nursed our sick
without women or running water;
bayonets ready, we entered the enemy's tents.

The Dog I Didn't Want

ran in anxious circles around the room—
stacked crates of dogs in need of homes.

I drifted toward a puppy, nonchalant;
the assistant said he hadn't, yet, been fixed,
and returned the dog I didn't want to his cage.

An older couple, looking to assuage
a recent loss, sat with a spaniel, transfixed.
The dog I didn't want yipped and cried

in his metal pen. "Take him for a walk,"
the keeper called, gave me a leash. Outside he stalked
the mailbox post and tugged to come inside.

He wouldn't meet my gaze or lick my hand
or charm with any doggy gifts. Instead,
the dog I didn't want curled up and tucked his head

into the coiled spiral of his body, color of sand.
Quiet, eyes closed, snout down, he awaited his fate
like one bound for the gallows or the chair.

Resigned, unloved, the dog I didn't want
in his despair won me his small estate.

Dyke

The word came after me, then hid each time
I turned to look at it.
It breathed in the hedge. I could hear it bite
and snap the air.

I feared the woman with slicked-back hair
sitting on a bar stool,
her back to the dance floor, a beer in her hands.
Disco drove the word away

but it came back: *Bulldyke, Bulldagger.*
What did the word want
with me, and why this dread, this desire, this
dangerous butch

striding through Kenmore Square
uncamouflaged?
Dyke had a spike in it, a cleated surge.
In leathers, the word leapt

eighteenth-century grillwork
on the Boston Common and led the parade
around the city,
the slow, snaking, joyful motorcade

of a new millennium. First
I had to hate her;
then I had to hurt her; the rest of my life,
I ate from her hand.

When You Look at the Spines of Your Books

for Amy Lang

arrayed around the rooms
you know who you are
as the diver knows herself
by the molecules of air
and water she displaces
carving her torso into form.

The typefaces and shiny patinas
where your fingers rubbed
the titles; the classrooms, the students,
the decades of civil strife;
here, demonstrators still chant and march.
Arguments take shape and you

draft a proposal, you protest in DC
When you look at the spines of your books
you know the arduous training of the mind
for clarity and compassion. You are Buddhist
and Hindu, Arab and Jew forever
having to learn the other,

shared climate and history of human
settlement, where alluvial sediment
preserved the striped clay fragments of a flute,
and the ethnographer recorded that
everyone for five hundred miles
knew the harmonies.

DOMAIN OF PERFECT AFFECTION

The New Egypt

I think of my father who believes
a Jew can outwit fate by owning land.
Slave to property now, I mow
and mow, my destiny the new Egypt.
From his father, the tailor, he learned not
to rent but to own; to borrow to buy.
To conform, I disguise myself and drag
the mower into the drive, where I ponder
the silky oil, the plastic casing, the choke.
From my father, I learned the dignity
of exile and the fire of acquisition,
not to live in places lightly, but to plant
the self like an orange tree in the desert
and irrigate, irrigate, irrigate.

Midsummer Count

Because there's a word, there's a way to wonder
if any of our group shagging baseballs
all spring might not have been a girl at all
but a hybrid cultivar. Micki and Jackie
resembled twin ponies, palomino
manes like vanilla frosting. Ruddy turnstones,
Sal and Les tumbled through the neighborhood,
grandstanding for screams. We all wanted to be
boys then, to serve the power we knew
found delight in our swinging from trees.
We wanted to serve the one god of joy
in the body and wreck ourselves at the altar
of summer nights on the city stoop, our shaped parts
sprouting overnight as we slept, changelings.
Sometimes I chose the hard singularity
of the young liege, honor bound even in defeat.
To the armor and scabbard I cleaved,
make-believe punishments a drubbing I took
to prove my manliness, my worthiness.
Sometimes I starred in my own
midsummer count and dreamed myself
a handsome specimen in bright plumage,
recognizable on the wing, most numerous
in early June when my kind crossed natural barriers.

Man of the Year

My father tells the story of his life

and he repeats *The most important thing:*
    to love your work.
I always loved my work. I was a lucky man.

This man who makes up half of who I am,
    this blusterer
who tricked the rich, outsmarting smarter men,

gave up his Army life insurance plan
    (not thinking of the future
wife and kids) and brokered deals with two-faced

rats who disappeared his cash but later overpaid
    for building sites.
In every tale my father plays outlaw, a Robin Hood

for whom I'm named, a type of yeoman
    refused admission
into certain clubs. For years he joined no guild—

no *Drapers, Goldsmiths, Skinners, Merchant*
    Tailors, Salters, Vintners—
but lived on prescience and cleverness.

He was the self-inventing Polish immigrant's
    son, transformed
by American tools into Errol Flynn.

As he speaks, I remember the phone calls
    during meals—
an old woman dead in apartment two-twelve

or burst pipes and water flooding rooms.
    Hatless,
he left the house and my mother's face

assumed the permanent worry she wore,
    forced to watch him
gamble the future of the semi-detached house,

our college funds, and his weekly payroll.
    Manorial halls
of Philadelphia his Nottingham,

my father fashioned his fraternity
    without patronage
or royal charters but a mercantile

swagger, finding his Little John, Tinker,
    and Allen-a-Dale.
Wholesalers, retailers, in time they resembled

the men they set themselves against.
    Each year they roast and toast
one member, a remnant of the Grocer's Feast

held on St. Anthony's Day, when brothers
	communed and dined
on swan, capon, partridges, and wine.

They commission a coat of arms, a song,
	and honor my father—
exemplary, self-made, without debt—

as Man of the Year, a title he reveres
	for the distinguished
peerage he joins, the lineage of merry men.

Against Pleasure

Worry stole the kayaks and soured the milk.
Now, it's jellyfish for the rest of the summer
and the ozone layer full of holes.
Worry beats me to the phone.
Worry beats me to the kitchen,
and all the food is sorry. Worry calcifies
my ears against music; it stoppers my nose
against barbecue. All films end badly.
Paintings taunt with their smug convictions.
In the dark, Worry wraps her long legs
around me, promises to be mine forever.

Thugs hijacked all the good parking spaces.
There's never a good time for lunch.
And why, my mother asks, *must you track*
beach sand into the apartment?
No, don't bother with books,
not reading much these days.
And who wants to walk the Boardwalk anyway,
with scam artists who steal your home and savings?
Watch out for talk that sounds too good to be true.
You, she says pointing at me,
don't worry so much.

A Pasture of My Palm

Trembling, desirous, above the display
case, I hovered with my child's hand. Beneath,
porcelain palominos stamped their feet,
and foals stood with their long legs splayed. I longed

to take one home, to place it on a shelf
and study the raised leg, the frothy mane.
Then, cupping the horse's shape in my hand,
I'd make a pasture of my palm, a field.

No one was looking, no one, I reasoned,
would know I'd swiped it, toy in my pocket.
That night I stroked the caramel china.
I was galloping, when my mother walked

into my room. She knew I was lying.
(*The horse? a gift* . . .) I cried when she told me
we'd speak with the manager the next day.
In his office I stood, wept, but even

then I was really crying for the cheap
horse back in the glass case, my mother,
my foolish and punishable desires,
the future taking shape: corral, stampede.

Salon

Acolyte at the font, my mother
bends before basin and hose
where Jackie soaps her fine head,
adjusting pressure and temperature.
How many times has she
bared her throat, her clavicle,
beside the other old women?
How many times the regular
cleansing and surrender to the cold chair,
the sink, the detergents, the lights,
the slick of water down the nape?
Turbaned and ready,
she forgoes the tray of sliced bagels
and donuts, a small, private dignity.

Vivienne, the manicurist, dispels despair,
takes my mother's old hands into her swift
hands and soaks them to soften
the cuticles before the rounding and shaping.
As they talk my mother attends
to the lifelong business of revealing
and withholding, careful to frame each story
while Vivienne lacquers each nail
and then inspects each slender finger,
rubbing my mother's hands
with the fragrant, thin lotion,
each summarizing her week, each
condemning that which must be condemned,
each celebrating the manicure and the tip.

Sometimes in pain, sometimes broken
with grief in the parking lot,
my mother keeps her Friday appointment
time protected now by ritual and tradition.

The fine cotton of Michael's white shirt
brushes against her cheek as they stare
into the mirror at one another.
Ennobled by his gaze, she accepts
her diminishment, she who knows herself
his favorite. In their cryptic language
they confide and converse, his hands busy
in her hair, her hands quiet in her lap.
Barrel-chested, Italian, a lover of opera,
he husbands his money and his lover, Ethan;
only with him may she discuss my lover and me,
and in this way intimacy takes the shape
of the afternoon she passes in the salon,
in the domain of perfect affection.

Borderline

in memory of Jill Wendy Becker, 1954–1987

    Brink, brow, verge, brim. I grew
adjacent and then away—leaving you, sister,

    on the margin of error, your uncultivated strip,
staring at coastlines where others converged.

    Not for you the adaptation, the going along, the realistic
expectation, the rules regarding performance

    in work or the timbre of friendship. Not for you
a rowboat with oars and oarlocks from which to paddle

    to mudflats and there encounter the stargazer
that buries itself in the muddy sand

    or the common shipworm that opens wood
and confounds the shipwright's carpentry.

    Oh, the co-housing arrangements of bivalves!
How they drill and devour each other,

    like us on the biochemical ledges
where your doctor knew no drug or medication

    to help fifteen years ago. You lived between
diagnoses, your illness nonspecific, placeless,

    and occupied your indeterminacy
not as protective coloration but condition,

    today characterized by some as trauma
in early development affecting brain function

    or an intrauterine factor
to which you were genetically predisposed.

    Certain patterns, some studies show,
of overinvolvement between parent and child

    may be causative factors. You tenanted
an invalidating space where sandbars rose

    and disappeared overnight, where organisms
are fragile and prone to rapid deterioration;

    thus, mind and place co-create each other
over time, and in you, magical thinker, impulsive

    brooder, both remained lawless,
mutable, labile. Neither barrier beach

    nor tide pool nor undersea meadow
could nourish you, as the rank estuary sustains

    the bottom-dwelling sea robin
that learns to walk on wing-shaped fins.

The Miniaturists

in memory of painter Donald Evans, 1945–1977

When she showed me the canceled stamps
    of Evans's imaginary
countries, their carved postmarks,

I thought how lovely to live in a nation
    he named *Stein*,
where, to celebrate the fiftieth anniversary

of *Tender Buttons*, the post office
    issued
stamps with quotations from the text.

She lauded his studies of pears, his love
    of appearances,
his taxonomies of seashells and palm trees

and took me, first, to fictitious *Nadorp*
    for the children's series,
stamps of paired objects, elusive meanings:

bow tie & rabbit; sunrise & comma.
    Whatever he loved, he loved
to scale, and then scaled down: an archipelago

of Friends and Lovers (*Amis et Amants*),
    or the state
named for the artist *Weisbecker*, in whose loft

he painted the homely *National Chair Works*—
    four chairs
in praise of Lower East Side hospitality.

She embraced her own treasures: World War I
    memorabilia, vintage lesbian
pulp fiction, insects in amber, recordings of Caruso.

Preserved like the cat mummy in the British Museum,
    the complete handwritten draft
of her dissertation stood in its portable sanctuary.

She'd take it from the tabernacle, part the silk wrapper,
    and show me the inscrutable
cross-hatchings, pages smelling of lemonwood.

Over dinner, we enjoyed watercolors of *Mangiare*,
    for which he named cities
after Italian dishes and created the region called *Pasta*,

composed of twenty-five provinces, commemorated
    on festive stamps
to philatelic standards, properly perforated.

When the affair ended, I walked each day
    to the tiny park
with the diminutive swing set and pumped

my enormous feet against the small sky.

Summer's Tale

Isn't the story better embellished?
Aren't we happier wooded and beached,
burnished with patina? Curved, mauved?
Take out the bee sting and emergency room,
the ungracious guest, the rainy weekends.
Aren't we better off trailing lilac streamers?
Pretend we take the Zakim Bridge at sunset,
halyards clank in Hingham Harbor as we toast.
Who could choose one god among all the bright
feathers of August or tell a summer story
without its old fishhooks and salt-weathered prospects?
I'll add the foreign stamps, the halogens;
you bring the clambake and watercolors.
Let's give the contractor a bit part in the kayak.

Island of Daily Life

in memory of Sandra Kanter, 1944–2004

This one is for Sandy
    who loves poems about ordinary things.
        For her, I'll keep my abstractions

    to a minimum and praise
the open carpentry of the summer cabins
    for their impromptu shelves

        where every ledge invites a wildflower bouquet
    or a drawing from a child at camp
or a special stone plucked from the lake,

    and I praise the lake
        with its dappled beach and sloping light,
    the comforting iterations

of rowboat, bathing cap, splash,
    where lakefront trees and small docks
        flare in the late afternoon, and a neighbor

    calls softly to her daughter, *it's time
to go, don't forget your things* . . .
    This poem gets up early for the Saturday

        yard sale and celebrates the evening
    walk across the mowing
through low-bush blueberries.

Sometimes guests from the city.
    Always the dog in his summer
haircut announcing his arrival.

This poem honors the poached fish and the beans,
    the goat cheese and the wine,
        the poems read aloud after dinner

    for their attention
to the quiddities, to aspects
    of our communal selves

    sheared of the theoretical.
This poem celebrates the passing
of the dish and the return of the bowl,

    the full moon now high
        above October lakes, shining
on a thousand forgotten beach books.

Head of an Angel

I've given up trying to decide
what Dürer intended and accept myself
for what I am—androgynous, sublime.

Staminate and pistillate, my flower's
immortal, and maybe that's the point
of the artist's invitation to look

at the stem of my sinuous neck,
the grey ink and white heightening
he brushed on my imperishable curls.

What I'm listening for, Venetian blue,
you infer from my upturned eyes, my mind
through which the mind of God is passing.

Late Butch-Femme

Long accustomed to playing the butch
I saw you for the femme I thought you were—
long waisted, well bred, the hostess who knew
to fold the napkin in the wineglass. But I had not
watched you square your shoulders before the arborist,
determined to take down the holly to save the oak.

No, you said, *the pin oak goes, the holly stays.*
The gutter man who wants his check will have
to repair the drain he botched. *Please have your son
call me*, you say, your fingers ready for another call.
In the cellar, among the foraged dressers, you measure
and sand and strip. Come up for the lunch I made you,
O handy lover, with your paint brushes bristling,
your small drill, your retractable blade.

Ok, Tucker

You win. My arm got tired of throwing the ball
before you got tired of scrambling up the river-
bank to fetch it. OK, Tucker, you can come, too.
Since you open the door with your clever snout
I'm not about to shove you back in. You win
the beauty contest, the most finicky eater award,
and the like-a-dog-with-a-bone prize; you win
the first-one-in-the-car sweepstakes. Look,
Tucker, we had no choice when we squared off
in your adolescence, we had to get along, it was a live-
and-let-live situation, both of us in love with her.
OK, I bribed you with biscuits and rides;
you conned me with a handshake and a smile.
Remember hide-and-seek in the cornfield,
the jack-in-the pulpit, the lady slipper?
That week at the beach with smelly gulls
wrapped in slime and tangled lines of seaweed?
And a pen of chickens? You had it made, but no!
Old girl, you chased the phantom squirrel
up the slope again and again, returned
slack-jawed, refused to come off the porch,
stood your ground in freezing November rain,
showed your dog's teeth when I showed my human
fear and for good measure ran circles around me—
when I was her woman, but you were her dog.

On Friendship

after Horace

Come down, M, stop sulking in that tree.
If the contractor came late and the workers shingling the barn
made a mistake, if the fuel tank in the truck's kaput, if your dead
friend's dog won't eat dinner,
pluck a few raspberries from the October garden.
OK, so you have to dig up the dahlias!

Still holding a grudge about that trip to Italy? Our bad sex life
after our good sex life? (Darling, must we return to the Tigris and Euphrates?)
After twenty years of friendship, we're still lousy
at talking to each other, two middle-aged women
in an age of nonpotable water on Long Island,
lethal viruses housed offshore, the scallop harvest at record lows.

Let me recommend Horace, who combined passion with a practical love
for the snafu, who accepted the bungler, the perfectionist, the one
who must have a pear-shaped glass with a narrow top
for aromatic liquors, the two-faced, the evasive, the worried.
He knew that friendship is neither intermittent, nor divisible
into parts, but aboriginal, discordant, the new music.

M, come down from that tree and listen to the apples
dropping on the tin roof. We've been friends since the cradle
of civilization, a pair of foragers watching the deer at midnight
sustain themselves on the rotten, the fallen.

With Two Camels and One Donkey

"Art does not reproduce the visible, it makes visible."
—*Paul Klee*

May we walk into our lives as into a watercolor,
grounded in sunlight, with two large ruminants and a baying ass.
May we go by foot, hot paving stones giving way to the Perfume Makers' Souk,
cajoling two camels and the small-hoofed donkey.
May we improvise mosaics in the maize and indigo plazas,
with our crazy families, over aqueducts made famous by warring
Romans, and through decaying archways,
followed by two camels and one disagreeable donkey.
May we jam in the amphitheater and read aloud our odes to friends
who will love and disappoint and delight us in the melodies of friendship,
remembering to water two camels and one obstinate donkey.
In blowing sand that stings our faces, with recollections of our dead tenderly
wrapped and shaped like pyramids, may we sway
rhythmically on the backs of two camels and one moody donkey.
May we cherish the desert and embrace our memories of the sea,
knowing that one does not cancel out the other
but permits a cobalt-blue feather to grow in the mind.
May we gather in temporary shelters and break bread with others,
never allowing our envy to get out of hand and respecting the laws
of the lands we cross on two camels and one petulant donkey.
Thus, the painter invented this fanciful checkerboard grid,
this landscape of magic squares into which we may walk
with our lives and our deaths, with two camels and one recalcitrant donkey.

THE HORSE FAIR

The Horse Fair

> My skirts would have been a great hindrance, making me
> conspicuous and perhaps calling forth unpleasant remarks.
>
> . . . Thus I was taken for a young lad, and unmolested.
>
> —ROSA BONHEUR

I

Found out, identified astride
the chestnut, head tilted
in the manner of the rearing

grey Percheron, you are
Rosa Bonheur disguised as one
of the handlers,

cross-dressed in a blue smock,
center of the painting.
You are performing a fantasy

of belonging
to a genre-scene that admits
none of your sex

and now the art history
that permitted you
to remain invisible

finds you androgynous
where horses bristle
at their restraining tack.

2

> There is in every animal's eye a dim image and gleam of humanity, a flash of strange light through which their life looks out and up to our great mystery of command over them.
>
> —JOHN RUSKIN

She would not see them as subservient.
She painted the tarsal joint of the hind leg
for forty years, perfecting its voluted spring.
She knew the Arabian horse to be of porphyry, granite, and sandstone;
she knew the English stallion Hobgoblin, veined with seawater.
She knew anatomical science predicted movement;
thus, in trousers and boots, through the slaughterhouses and stockyards
and livestock markets, a small woman with cropped hair passed.
She knew the Belgian, her dense ossature, wattage of the livid eye,
oscillation of gait, the withheld stampede gathering
in the staunch shoulder for the haulage of artillery.
She would not picture subservience.

3

The taxonomies enclose and divide
Rosa, lover of science, Rosa, lover of Nathalie and Anna
I am she who asked permission to dress
as a man and had my physician countersign

for reasons of health so I could go forth
into my own country and abroad to study
Scottish sheep and oxen at The Falkirk Fair
I drew their bodies swimming

across the firth at Loch Leven
where drovers in small boats guided
the great beasts struggling up the banks
their sleek heads rose dripping

4

> Mlle. Rosa paints almost like a man.
> —THÉOPHILE THORÉ

The oxen configure an immense mute horizon
with the bunkers of their bodies.

Lustrous in the sun they furrow
the ground and plough their shadows under.

Across sienna trenches, uptilted,
they labor two abreast, fissures of skin

greased with oil. Headdresses of horns point.
This was her choice: heavy blade at the end

of the beam, draft teams dwarfing the human
figure, tiny as a painted lead soldier.

5

> I have a veritable passion, you know, for this unfortunate race and I deplore that it is disappearing before the White usurpers.
>
> —ROSA BONHEUR

Cody sold *the unfortunate race* to England and France
as the *real* west in *actual scenes*
of slaughters in which he bragged he had taken part
we do not know—the facts
surrounding his life are uncertain

but not the promotional posters with Red Shirt
and Rosa Bonheur
given permission to draw in the thirty-acre field
where performers camped
between staged conquests Cody presented as *civilizing*

A chronicle of despair said Black Elk who joined
The Rough Riders to mend the broken
hoop of history   In the portrait Bonheur painted
Cody rides a white horse, sits tall in fringed buckskin
on playbills and postcards

They say he was not entirely pleased with the likeness
and had his head repainted

6

I strove to comprehend the soul
of Fathma, my lioness
reclining with her on a straw mat
studying her eye in many drawings

I stocked my stables with Icelandic
ponies, goats and yaks
Elk roamed the grounds and sometimes I
was summoned by the Empress

as I worked from a plaster cast
of a gazelle or a stuffed hawk
or played with Boniface the monkey
who liked to take my hand and walk

7

The taxonomies enclose and divide
They said I was a Jew
from Bordeaux
and called me Rosa Mazel-Tov

before I died famous on the lip
of the twentieth century
Numerous the forged engravings, the collaborating
dealers, the pirated prints

of *The Horse Fair*, the notebooks
carrying my studio stamp and the stories
of a critic discovering me
in a frock coat, trousers, spurs, queer hat.

8

> Now I am turned 73 and have only one tooth left
> wherewith to snarl at humanity.
>
> —ROSA BONHEUR

Nine horses running in a cadenced score,
their unshod hooves thresh the wheat and the thresher's whip
like a high note on the unfinished canvas.

An immense dream of balance, gallop, and pivot—
without bridle or harness—
the picture hung for thirty years in the atelier.

She wanted to show the fire that blows
from the horses' nostrils, and the driven herd mutinous, rising
and falling along the enclosure of the thresher's will

into the foundry of weight and motion
where metal melts and pours into horse.
Dangerous as fission the arson of their turning;

tails flare behind obdurate haunches, chests brace in disavowal.
She painted the intelligence of dished faces resisting—
her life's project their refusal.

Life Forms

When a whale rolls ashore
the villagers know a drowned person
is coming home
who may have started life
as a halibut, shucked tail and fins
for a musher's lot.
If she's going to die soon,
a woman may hear the owl call her name.
A screech owl is a person
punished for speaking out of turn.
I didn't know the canoe
in the museum
had been a two-headed sea serpent
the Kwakiutl fed with seals.
I didn't know that raven's wings
could open to reveal
a human head.
A woman washing in a stream refused
to come when her husband called.
Her leather apron slapped the shore,
became a tail. She grew thick fur
and slipped from her marriage
disguised as a beaver.

We stopped at Nenana to place our bets
on the exact minute of the ice breakup.
I wanted to see the clock that stops
when the ice goes out.
I wanted to see the salmon-man
who pumps gas at the filling station,
forced into the human world
after leaping upriver.

The Wood Lot

for Victor Kumin

In the farmhouse, early morning,
you review the list of chores
tacked to the post. They vary by season,

site, number of hands needed,
number of trips, machinery
and vehicles. Tasks fall into invisible

subcategories—the urgent,
the accidental, the rock-bound.
We walk uphill, you're explaining

citizenship, your passion for the civic work
that builds a library, a community,
a two-hundred-year-old stone wall.

We spend an hour stacking wood,
a companionable chore, good for two,
you tell me, never one alone.

Alone, the stacker will grow careless, miss
the logs' listing tendency, forget to throw
halves aside for supporting ends. You shim

unsteady places as we go, selecting
pieces for the trim, crisp line
that gives us room for another row.

You are love's year-round
caretaker, and by your example I understand
the artfulness of love's responsibilities.

Phaeton

for Maxine Kumin

He sees the light cart in the paddock,
isn't thinking of the time he spooked a month ago—
the cart half-hitched, the gate unlocked—
and you held on. Today he's calm,

standing quietly as you thread the traces through
the footman's loop and ask him to back up. I stand
by his Arab head, masked in mosquito netting, and then
join you in the seat that substitutes, today, for his back.

Easy in your hands, he trots up the road, ears alert
to your voice, the encouraging praise, the clucks that urge him
past laziness when the hill steepens. Your hands know
the give and take of the canter, the sweet compromise

that adjudicates his power and your will. In our helmets,
under these summer trees, we are as safe as we will ever be.

The Donor

for Richard Mihelcic

He was the largest man I'd ever seen.
Sun glittered behind him on new leaves. He shook
our hands. "My son was just a college kid who turned
special at the end; I learned, praise God, so much. . . ."
Who is this man? I wondered in his plush DC office,

where we sat rapt before his story like students,
not teachers on a fund-raising errand,
part condolence call. I remembered the thin
young man and his poems that lacked concrete detail,
while his father hurried on, steering us

through the molecular compositions
that would not stay the stridor issuing
from the boy's lungs, the streptozotocin
that wiped out insulin-producing cells,
the boy's heroic sadness, season of gurneys.

Had my father ever unburdened himself
to a stranger? After my sister took her life
he stared, spent, from a room darkened by shame,
silent. The donor divested himself of secrets,
made public his desperate transactions:

in the sub-basement at Hopkins, on the Volga River in winter,
he wrapped his boy in a blanket, in a nineteenth-century novel,
for a twenty-first century procedure.
His sentences coursed into Chekhovian time, while I
pondered the carriage driver in "The Lament,"

overcome by his son's death, seeking someone
to listen to his tale. In the end, he tells his horse
his threnody. And though we were strangers
to him, Matthew's father described how the doctors broke
his son's ribs to get at his heart, how, wasted

by liver failure, he hung on, every antibiotic
active against tumors blackening his body.
He conjured a language in which machines conversed,
wept, asked forgiveness, obsessed with the telling
details. And when he saw we were crying,

he asked our permission to continue
through the damaged corridors
through the Valley of the Shadow of Death and up
to the ICU and the months of shunts
and feeding tubes, to the empty stomach

at the end of the world. The substrata of menace.
There, he named names—doctors compassionate and harsh—
who bought Matt time while he was dying. Once, when the boy was close
to death, he fed him, for the taste, chocolate
ice cream. Then pumped it out.

"My son was just a kid grown magnificent
by dying." He wiped his brow. "Thanks for coming."
This father, shot through with love and grief,
secured his son's ordeal in us, transfusion
of words. The donor's money will fund a prize

each year. And what shall we do with this fearful
story of one man's suffering but shine and polish it
with our own additions and subtractions? What shall we subsidize
with our sorrows after the morning meeting,
all of our assets liquid as tears?

Raccoon

With his two hands
    covering his two eyes
        he prays in the middle of the road

over the clump of fur and bone
    that was himself.
        He looks like my old *zayde*

in the synagogue
    two decades ago
        ashamed for his poverty.

Comedian of the hard frost,
    deft champion of screw-on tops,
        more than once we met

over the garbage of daily life—
    you poised on the proscenium
        of a metal lid,

me caught in the isosceles
    of an upstate porch light.
        For forty years my grandfather stitched

linings into women's suits
    under a searchlight the shop foreman hung
        over the old man's head.

Sometimes he slapped his son with his hat
    when he got home and cursed his boss
        for making him sew on the Sabbath.

Not even a coat will be made of you,
    brother raccoon, you who did not outlive
        this year's bachelor's buttons and marigolds,

who secured whatever flesh
    you could find and made your way
        dragging your black-ringed tail

across the collaborating streets at dawn
    where the local truckers
        in their shiny rigs stop at nothing.

Wants

Two Jewish kids among Protestants,
    we knew to stand up for the other,
        though we wanted something we each couldn't get:

I wanted the smart, athletic girls
    on the varsity squad, their confidences, their blue book bags
        leaning against my leg in study hall;

you wanted to be thin, to get a Gentile boyfriend,
    a normal boy from public school who'd make you swoon.
        Nights, you tapped a long finger on the cannister of pot

you hid in your dresser, and we laughed until I got paranoid or sad.
    Lighten up, you'd say. *Soon we'll be out of this hell hole.*
        When your brother came home, he rooted for money

in every room, finally jumped you for your wallet. *No!* you screamed
    as he ran—high on meth—to his Triumph, taking
        the bills and tossing your wallet on the lawn.

King of shopping centers, your grandfather *made more money*
    in a year than most make in a lifetime, my mother said.
        Your brother wrecked three cars, you went to diet camp.

We didn't speak for twenty-five years,
    and then you tracked me down. How our dead from that town
        have accumulated, Ellen! So many dead! The German

Jews who turned away from their Russian cousins
> lie in the ground with them now. They join the shopping center Jews
>> and the tailor Jews, the Jews driven mad, like my sister,

and your dreadful mother whose money came to you,
> who would have preferred her love, instead. Your brother—
>> tracks up his arms, houses gone, deficits actionable—borrows

against the estate, sues the trustees.
> What else is new? A second husband and a son, the quiet view
>> from the window, nothing I would have expected of you.

You can't always get what you want, Mick Jagger sang.
> We did not know our history and class
>> would stockade us, until illness or bad luck.

Years ago, in blue tunics, the volleyball captains chose sides
> and we suffered to watch the choosing, to see
>> who would be picked last. Sometimes you. Sometimes me.

Elegy for a Secular Man

I

He lived in the days he fabricated
    with *retablos* and *santos* and painted Acoma pots
        he bought in 1951 at the Santo Domingo Feast Day
            a six-hour drive from Taos over dirt
                with his lovers, men uncertain
                      about Henry and his falling-down adobe

and his plan to dwell in that dry conquered country
    Anglo among the spirits of the Basket Makers
        among the Penitente and the suspicious
            Like the forsaken desert broken into angular planes
                he wore his brokenness his rage his respect his secularism
                    he drove the Bookmobile to every parish in the county

2

I know who you are
   and I know who I am
      I'm just not sure where we are
         he said in the nursing home
            under the fluorescence
            He slowly pulled his wrist-
            watch to his face and said
               seven-thirty
               but one isn't certain
               if that means morning or evening
            He nodded to the window
it only matters in that world

3

Henry watched from his aluminum folding chair
    as they danced he studied their beaded moccasins
and heard the bells and tortoise shells and deer hooves
    clank and sing against the men's bodies
streaked with white paint and sweat

Among the dancers moved the clowns who stooped to tie
    a headdress or massage a dancer's cramp
Like mothers they shepherded the dancing children
    one lost   one out of line   feminized by their function
never losing their great power said Henry

4

In the painting of the procession,
storm clouds bear down
like blocks of ingots—

gauntlet gray, gunmetal gray.
And the false dusk almost
shadows the foregrounded hills,

pewter under snow. There, the cortege
winds, serpentine, as figures follow
one another like pack ponies,

over poor footing,
in the narrow space
the painter reserved for mourners,

unaware of the hole he cut
in the marbled cloud cover
where a spot of blue burns through.

5

When his hearing went he shouted *The liver is the most diseased part*
    of the animal in line at Furr's cafeteria before the opera
        I'll have the liver, please he crooned The smell of sage blew
            through the open windows after *The Magic Flute*
                What's the matter with this company? he roared
                    Their voices get fainter every year

He lived in rooms made complex by the patterns
    of Navajo rugs named for old trading posts
        Two Grey Hills Crystal Germantown
            cochineal stripes draped chair and bed
                cobalt crosses pictograph of cow and horse
                saddle blanket stained with use

6

Diapered and sweet-smelling he lay
on the hospital bed *This isn't exactly the Waldorf, honey*
he said, humming an ostinato

O my drag queen my Communist my Jew
We know the dignity in self-effacement
the mockery the erasure the devastating remark

Now your brain cannot control your bowels
I pull the diaper from your ankles and leave you
on the toilet   I will bring the attendant

to clean you up while I wait in the lobby
learning the illiberal limits of my love
in this afterlife of the body

In Praise of the Basset Hound

This unlovely dog, with warts, and a terrible stink
common to the breed, legless as a walrus, teaches me
to pursue my life with devotion. Steadfast enthusiast
of fisher cat and vole, she relies now almost entirely on scent
and sings her hound's song of pleasure when we come
close enough for her to hear her name.
In snow above her shoulder, she tracks our skis,
when all we can see is her metronome tail
tipped in black, sweeping the horizon a mile back.
We keep her, incontinent, in an old shed behind the farmhouse,
a wire fence around her run. Warm days, nose in the air,
she sits like an old retiree in the sun, listening
to warblers build their spring nests.
Her warts ooze, her eyes rain green phlegm. Still,
I kiss her and hold her against my breast,
she who whelped twelve litters before someone
took pity and bought her from the breeder.
Never permitted to lick hand or face, she will not
disgrace her training and extend her tongue in play,
though I offer my cheek. Daily, she shows me
the meaning of character, loping painfully
on swollen paws. I apply salve to her scaley folds,
croon over her. Who among us has not been
moved by the magnificence of mute
creatures in their abundant, dying skin?

Late Words for My Sister

You did not want to remember
    with me how he raged up the stairs
        unbuckling the black leather

strap we called the belt.
    How our four thin legs danced
        up and down on the bed like

the jointed limbs of marionettes
    while the burning lariat of his anger
        seared our legs; how his face blazed and his eyes

glowed as he took the whip back in a tight
    circle to strike again. And again. We begged him to stop.
        Remember? And when he relented, panting like an animal

that has run a great distance, he paused, and we could see
    the sweat on his lip and under his arms. He hung there,
        his bulk suspended from his shoulders

by a power greater than he, and as we crept past him
    he slapped me, hard across the face, sparing you
        that humiliation

because you were weak and the youngest
    and had only followed my example into evildoing.
        I tried to make myself small, to pass him, or no,

I'm remembering wrong. Maybe I sneered. Maybe
    I had not yet learned to cower before the bully,
        to bare my neck, to admit when I had lost.

How surprised you would be to see him now,
    an old man checking the price
        of milk at the supermarket against

the price in his head. The difference
    is a conundrum, a fracture in continuity,
        the way his daughters broke from his plan.

In the Days of Awe

for Abbe, Sally, and Joseph

I Amidah

Hear my personal prayer, *the words of my mouth and the meditation
of my heart* that I may find a way back through love
In the hospital room packed in blood-soaked cotton the new mother lay
animal-exhausted technicians whisked the child away in the first
hours there was fear O teach me to withhold judgment

of the one who took my place who said *yes* when I said *no*
whose days opened to the child when my days foreclosed
she who conceived of joy where I imagined the crossbar
against my chest subjugation of family life the double
harness the never-ending tasks the clamp and vise

II Shofar

The *shofar* blasts birthday of the world of our dominion
over nature in the Kingdom of the Lord our God Ruler
of the Universe Then why am I weeping into this tissue?
What is this child to me who refused to stay and raise him?
What is this broken covenant, this yoke?

III Tashlikh

By a small stream as is customary
we cast into the water with its drift
of leaves our quarrels like stones our envies
and resentments *O Lord You do not maintain anger
but delight in forgiveness*

V Aleinu

You take me down to the nursery to see
Joseph in his little cap of many colors
with his jaundice and his brisk efficient keepers
Will you be kind? *Cleanse my mind of wickedness
Teach me to attain a heart of wisdom*

In the synagogue the families praise *all fruit-bearing trees
and cedars all wild beasts and cattle* I watch a woman
and her teenage daughter confer lean into each other
They hold the *mahzor* between them their mouths shape the beautiful
Hebrew I do not know how to read except in transliteration

V Teshuvah

Turn from evil and do good the Psalmist says turning
Round the turn turn the key clock the turn turn in time
time to turn words into footsteps to lead the young colt to the field
to turn from the old year the old self You are ready
to turn and be healed only face only begin

VI Amidah

Inscribe him in the Book of Life for Your sake   living God
She opened up the book of her body again and again
She would not stop trying though I mocked her   a year
ended and a year began   I had no imagination for family life
inhabiting sadly that place for years

Inhabiting sadly that place for years   with me   who chose
to keep my faith with those who sleep in dust   she chose
against the quiet house and noiseless rooms she chose
to bear her mortal woman's share and split her life in two
or three or four   she said *I know what you want I want more*

VII Avinu malkeinu

Avinu malkeinu inscribe us in the Book of Deliverance
Avinu malkeinu inscribe us in the Book of Merit
Avinu malkeinu inscribe us in the Book of Forgiveness
Sarah beseeched God for a child and brought forth Isaac
And Sally brought forth Joseph   *Amen*

A voice commands the lightning that cleaves stones
A voice shatters stately cedars
A voice twists the trees and strips the forest bare
The devout say *In your love for your neighbor will you find God*
They say *Days are scrolls   Write only what you want remembered*

VIII Kedushah

We believe that God abides in mystery in a diaspora of dust
in the obsessive   the compulsive   the disordered   in the lonely
in the bosses   in the unendurable   in the technological
and pharmaceutical failures   in the very old
in the newborn   in memory   in kindness   in acts of loving kindness

We believe that God abides in the unfit   in those unshielded
by luck or faith and by bad luck made abject by the unctuous
I believe in the uncomputerized and the demoralized
the belittled and benumbed gazing like dumb beasts
like my sister groping mid-seizure back to speech

IX Mourner's Kaddish

Bless my sister who could not endure   bless her failure to thrive
and bless my parents in their magnificent witness
Sanctify this *Day of Remembrance   Grant them peace*
from the clichéd language of condolence cards   Be merciful to those
who passed *Your blessed days* in a curtained room of shame

In the public place   in the hall outfitted with a simple ark
the mourners stand   *Whom shall I dread?* we ask with our private
dreads on our civic faces   We are an assembly of stunned
children called to recite *Yit-gadal ve-yit kadash shmei raba*
There is always someone to mourn   Look around

X The Fast of Yom Kippur

Look around the congregation atones we certify regret
we recall our transgressions and those who transgressed against us
Where is my milk? Joseph cries and she feeds him   The Torah
teaches repentance   I remember my *zayde*, a shrunken man
at the front of the *shul* fasting By the last *Aleinu* he could not stand

My father brought smelling salts   the son who did not know
the prayers sat with his father   *His life was one long prayer
to the hereness of God*   On the maternity floor food and flowers
Choose life! shouts baby Joseph tightly bound in a cotton blanket
I'm afraid it's time to go says the kind nurse after visiting hours

XI Selihot

The days of women and men are as grass.
They flourish as flowers in the field.
The wind passes over them and is gone,
and no one can recognize where they grew.

XII *Amidah*

Inscribe for me a childless life   O lift me
to the Book of Many Forms that I might find another way
to honor my father and mother   their agony of bereavement
Let me understand the girl child I was   beloved as Joseph in his coat
of many colors, favored by his father   hated by his brothers

and by his brothers thrown into the pit   Then to live among strangers
in Egypt far from family   Bind me to these friends and to this child
that I may learn my true relation to the people of this story
Sanctify difference and refusal   bless
the lesbians   the child with two mothers   *Amen*

Sisters in Perpetual Motion

Urban wanderers,
    unhoused and unhinged, they are rapt in
        a perpetual motion of paraphernalia

trundling from Kendall to Central, Harvard to Porter.
    One in a gentleman's greatcoat—
        worsted gabardine and fur collar—

holds a sidebar conference with herself, pushes her metal
    shopping cart, argues with the invisible
        censorious judge of Mass Ave.

Parallel to traffic, she retains a centrifugal
    relationship to the lanes she occupies, strides
        away from the main, parent axis of rotation,

abjures public transportation or charity and returns,
    early evening, cold, coincident with those of us
        not charged with a conundrum of streets.

She sleeps in undocumented doorways and on grates and
    in neighborhood parks on benches and propped
        on soiled cushions she pushes.

Sponge of pocked foam bedding. Torn lining of a brown coat.
    Thus I remember my sister, her unbuilt days
        of compulsive walking before she decamped

to clinics and psych wards. Her walkabouts. Her unfettered speech.
    Her terrorist phone calls and the tyranny
        of her jurisdiction: thus, beleaguered,

she engineered a siege and won. *Timber up a frame dwelling,*
    I said. *Explain yourself to yourself.* In the end,
        the cops broke down the door of an empty house to find her.

Sad Sestina

for Susanna Kaysen

Today's sadness is different from yesterday's:
more green in it, some light rain, premonition of departures
and the unpacking of books and papers. *It's not a bad thing
to be sad*, my friend Susanna says. *Go with it.* I'm going by foot
into this sadness, the way we go as children into the awful
school day and the hours of cruelty and misunderstanding,

the way we go into family, into the savagery of standing
up for ourselves among siblings and parents, in yesterday's
living room, where secrecy turns to habit and we learn the awful,
unthinkable fact: time twists our days into a series of departures.
When he was mad, my father used to say, *Someone's got to foot
the bills*, and I think of him now, this man who knew one thing

for sure: you had to pay your own way, since nothing
came for free in this life. A young dyke, grandstanding
before the relatives, I held my sadness close, one foot
already out the door. Who could believe in yesterday's
homilies while women cruised me, seventeen and hot for departure?
Today's sadness unfurls without drama, without the awful

punishments or reprisals of that house. In its place, the awful,
simple, mystery of human melancholy. Most days, I'd trade anything
to be rid of the blues, accustomed to flight and departure,
strategies that saved my life. Today I'm befriending it, standing
beside my sadness like a pal down on her luck, who knows yesterday
isn't always a good predictor for tomorrow. A rabbit's foot

won't help; when the time comes, it's a question of putting my foot
in the stirrup and riding the sad horse of my body to the awful
little stable at the edge of town. And there to wait while yesterday
has its way with time. Susanna said, *To be sad is not a bad thing*,
and I believe her, as I pull the heavy saddle from the standing
horse and hang the bridle away. Sadness readies for my departure,

and I for hers. In a most unlikely departure
from the ordinary, even the tough butch on a bike will be a tenderfoot
when it comes to goodbyes. We carry on, notwithstanding
all the good times gone and December's awful
cheerfulness. Susanna, if I ever discern something
useful about sadness, I'll wish I'd known it yesterday.

I've put distracting things aside and discovered, underfoot,
no wisdom absent yesterday. Still, a saint would find this awful:
a standing date with change, a season of departures.

Adult Child

Now that my parents are old, they love me fiercely,
and I am grateful that the long detente of my childhood
has ended; we stroll through the retirement community.
My father would like to call the woman who left me
and tell her that I will be a wealthy woman someday.
We laugh, knowing she never cared about money
but patiently taught him to use his computer and program
the car phone. In the condo, my mother navigates
a maze of jewelry, tells me the history of watches,
bracelets, rings, pearls. She says I may sell
most of it, she just wants me to know what's what.
I drive her to the bank where we sign a little card
and walk, accompanied, into the vault, gray boxes
stacked like bodies. *Here*, she says, *are the titles and deeds.*

Against Silence

Silence is a meadow, guileless, gesturing with indigenous
grasses and wild flowers. Walk into it and the bees rise.
Silence is the thousand-leaved woods in rain,
New England turned jungly, fungal, a grid of humidity
where insects swarm around our martyred heads.

Silence is a game of dodgeball at dusk—
a matter of time until someone knocks you out
of the circle of bodies. I used to sway alone, slow
motion, the ball floating past my chest. Eyes in my hands,
eyes in the small of my back, I could anticipate the blow

and dodge it, schooled in the feint, the simulation.
Silence is the Old City of partition and quarter,
where a colonial fog blots the sun. And all the charm of the regime
hurried away, into museums: see the gold ear plugs?
the short musket with the flaring muzzle?

I want to hear the circular saw rotating at high speed,
excoriation, whine, orchestration of birds. Describe the sexual practices
of several Peruvian cultures. Harpsichord me. Entail me. Depose me.
The dangerous meadow shuts down at night.
The moon, rabbinical, mutters a prayer.

Why We Fear the Amish

Because they are secretly Jewish and eat matzoh on Saturday.
Because they smell us in fellowship with the dead works
of darkness and technology. Because we doubt ourselves.
We find their clothing remorseless; we find their beards unsanitary.
Who among us is not ashamed, speeding, to come upon a poor
horse pulling a cart uphill, everyone dressed the same?
We believe in the state and they believe in the button.

With their fellow Pennsylvanians, the Quakers, they hold noisy pep rallies.
They know the quilting bee, the honey bee and the husking bee
are the only proper activities for women.
Even their horses are thrifty and willing to starve for Christ.
In the Poconos, the men vacation with Hassidim and try on
each other's coats. Back home, no tractors with pneumatic tires.
Pity the child who wants a radio and must settle for a thermos.

When the world shifts to Daylight Savings Time, there's no time
like slow time, to stay out of step. In Standard Time
their horses trot faster than ours, for the Amish
set their clocks ahead. In January, they slaughter the animals.
In March, they go to the sales. In April, they plant potatoes.
In June, they cut alfalfa. In August, they cut alfalfa again.
In October, they dig potatoes. In December, they butcher and marry.

They modify the milk machine to suit the church, they change
the church to fit the chassis, amending their lives with hooks-and-eyes.
Their dress is a leisurely protest against chairmindedness.
We know their frugality in our corpulence. We know their sacrifice
for the group in our love for the individual. Our gods are
cross-dressers, nerds, beach bums, and poets. They know it.
By their pure walk and practice do they eye us from their carts.

The Monarchs of Parque Tranquilidad

On the ruins of Synagogue Cheva Bikur, built in 1887,
my neighbors fashioned Parque Tranquilidad
and adorned the gate with blue morning glories,

nimble gymnasts scaling the parallel bars.
I take the brick path to the Spanish Colonial toolshed,
to the bird bath studded with tiles—

our altarpiece—where a wooden Saint Francis
of Assisi oversees all immigrants in the Folk
Art style that dominates visual culture on 4th Street,

as in the commemorative portraits of Emilio and Mike,
painted on the north wall of Casa Mia—
young men who stopped expecting anything and now smile

at stock boys catching a smoke in the park, and single
mothers hurrying their kids to the Catholic school
on Sixth, and the homeless novelist who sets up his portable

typewriter beneath the Ornamental Cherry.
Below their large faces, the muralist wrote,
They are in heaven now.

Today in Parque Tranquilidad, heaven arrives as orange
monarchs, hundreds covering the purple fronds
of the butterfly bush with an involuntary, sexual broadcast

of desire. They linger above the imperial flowers and rush
to embrace them, beating their wings
in a syncopation I cannot fathom, though I stand

for a long time, staring at these migratory,
paper-thin creatures
and the painted faces of the dead boys of 4th Street.

Angels of the Lower East Side

Chico paints the dead of the East Village.
Like God he shows his hand but not his face.
On my street he left us Lilal, hurled from a meteor,
swaddled in the flag of Puerto Rico against a brick galaxy
painted black-and-white. *He couldn't support his habit*

the stock boy tells me. *Killed himself.*
Lilal in a swirling halo, from his eternal place
on the wall of his father's bodega, knows
I'm new here, winks at me behind the enchilada cart,
says *Soon you'll be Puerto Rican*, though I miss the synagogue

that became Iglesia Pentecosto del Divino Maestro
and wander the streets the way I traipsed the ghetto in Venice
in search of Italy's deported Jews. Out of respect
for their friend's son, the 4th Street card players set up the game
where Lilal can oversee their bids, where Chico strides,

invisible Holy Ghost in his gallery of angels.
Next to his portrait of Princess Diana, he painted Elisa,
the child *killed by her mother's boyfriend.* Word on the street
says the city's to blame and the caseworker who failed
to act on complaints. Elisa wears a pink parka, she has

olive skin, the somber eyes and dark hair of the revolutionary
she might have become, standing with the tall
nationalist in his black beret, long raincoat and heavy glasses,
hawking the worker's paper in Spanish outside the supermarket,
rain dripping down his face. In the subway,

wiping his glasses, his pile of unsold papers beside him,
he reminds me of my old friends selling *The Militant*, 1969.
On Houston Street, the young Latina singer, Selina, glances
away, suspicious of her manager, her maid, her fans.
Taken out by someone in her own production company.

We're standing by the liquor store, three doors down
from Iglesia San Isidro y Leandro, another church
that used to be a *shul*. He's waiting for the 14 Bus,
I'm waiting for Elisa and Selina to stop
insisting on their tragedies. I'm waiting for Chico

to explain Diana in expensive pearls against the glittering
background of stars. Chico says *Think of her sons*
and hightails it to the Williamsburg Bridge.
Why can't I escape Diana's bright teeth or forget
Elisa's pink coat, Selina's pursed red lips?

Lilal says *The dead will always be with us—
in the Jews who inhabited these streets, in those who perished
from typhus, in the violence of the father, in the violence of the tenement,
in the removal of the Star from the round window, in the violence of crack,
in the florid graffiti, in the faces painted on these walls.*

ALL-AMERICAN GIRL

Shopping

If things don't work out
I'll buy the belt
with the fashionable silver buckle
we saw on Canyon Road.
If we can't make peace
I'll order the leather duster and swagger
across the plaza in Santa Fe,
cross-dressing for the girls.
If you leave I'll go back
for the Navaho blanket
and the pawn ring, bargain
with the old woman who will know
I intend to buy.
If you pack your things,
if you undress in the bathroom,
if you see me for what I am,
I'll invest in the folk art mirror
with the leaping rabbits
on either side, I'll spring
for the Anasazi pot with the hole
in the bottom where the spirit
of the potter is said to escape
after her death.

If you say you never intended
to share your life, I'll haunt the museum
shops and flea markets,
I'll don the Spanish riding hat,
the buckskin gloves with fringe at the wrists,
I'll step into the cowboy boots
tanned crimson and designed to make
any woman feel like she owns the street.
If you never touch me again,
I'll do what my mother did
after she buried my sister:
outfitted herself in an elegant suit
for the rest of her life.

The Crypto-Jews

This summer, reading the history of the Jews of Spain,
I learned Fra Alfonso listed "holding philosophical discussions"
as a Jewish crime. I think of the loud fights
between me and my father when he would scream that only a Jew
could love another Jew. I love the sad proud history
of expulsion and wandering, the Moorish synagogue walled
in the Venetian ghetto, persistence of study and text.
If we are the old Christ-killers on the handles of walking sticks,
we've walked the earth as calves, owls, and scorpions.
In New Mexico, the descendants of Spanish *Conversos* come forth
to confess: tombstones in the yard carved with Stars of David,
no milk with meat, generations raised without pork.
What could it mean, this Hebrew script,
in grandmother's Catholic hand? Oh, New World, we drift
from eviction to eviction, go underground,
emerge in a bark on a canal, minister to kings, adapt to extreme
weather, peddle our goods and die into the future.

My Grandmother's Crystal Ball

Each summer we left Philadelphia
where our sweltering fathers swore they could drive their Falcons
around the rim of William Penn's fedora—a cast iron
version of their own—gigantic
and burning like a foundry in July.

Silver swells rolled forward like machinery
all day on the beach where we ran, five girl cousins too old
to be naked to the waist and wild as boys.
Late afternoon, the shadows of the great hotels
painted the sand.

After dark, our grandmother told us,
the water reached out predatory fingers and pulled
children under. Holding her hand, I heard hot, Dionysian laughter
rise from a blanket and saw the sandy, suntanned legs
of girls who sprinted up the stairs,

outlined by neon ads for peanuts and piers
that would, in a few years, disappear from Atlantic City.
I watched the sultry girls dash across the Boardwalk
and drop to the street. My cousins yawned
and my grandmother's eyes met mine—

as if she knew that I was already running
with the wrong crowd,
as if she could see me leaning
against a polished banister, staring
at a woman and letting her stare at me.

A History of Sexual Preference

We are walking our very public attraction
through eighteenth-century Philadelphia.
I am simultaneously butch girlfriend
and suburban child on a school trip,
Independence Hall, 1775, home
to the Second Continental Congress.
Although she is wearing her leather jacket,
although we have made love for the first time
in a hotel room on Rittenhouse Square,
I am preparing my teenage escape from Philadelphia,
from Elfreth's Alley, the oldest continuously occupied
residential street in the nation,
from Carpenters' Hall, from Congress Hall,
from Graff House where the young Thomas
Jefferson lived, summer of 1776. In my starched shirt
and waistcoat, in my leggings and buckled shoes,
in postmodern drag, as a young eighteenth-century statesman,
I am seventeen and tired of fighting for freedom
and the rights of men. I am already dreaming of Boston—
city of women, demonstrations, and revolution
on a grand and personal scale.
                Then the maître d'
is pulling out our chairs for brunch, we have the
surprised look of people who have been kissing
and now find themselves dressed and dining
in a Locust Street townhouse turned café,
who do not know one another very well, who continue

with optimism to pursue a relationship. *Eternity*
may simply be our mortal default mechanism
set on *hope* despite all evidence. In this mood,
I roll up my shirtsleeves and she touches my elbow.
I refuse the seedy view from the hotel window.
I picture instead their silver inkstands,
the hoopskirt factory on Arch Street,
the Wireworks, their eighteenth-century herb gardens,
their nineteenth-century row houses restored
with period door knockers.
Step outside.
We have been deeded the largest landscaped space
within a city anywhere in the world. In Fairmount Park,
on horseback, among the ancient ginkgoes, oaks, persimmons,
and magnolias, we are seventeen and imperishable, cutting classes
May of our senior year. And I am happy as the young
Tom Jefferson, unbuttoning my collar, imagining his power,
considering my healthy body, how I might use it in the service
of the country of my pleasure.

Solar

The desert is butch, she dismisses your illusions
about what you might do to make your life
work better, she stares you down and doesn't say
a word about your past. She brings you a thousand days,
a thousand suns effortlessly each morning rising.
She lets you think what you want all afternoon.
Rain walks across her mesa, red-tailed hawks
writhe in fields of air, she lets you look at her.
She laughs at your study habits, your orderly house,
your need to name her "vainest woman you've ever met."
Then she turns you toward the voluptuous valleys,
she gives you dreams of green forests,
she doesn't care who else you love.
She sings in the grass, the sagebrush, the small trees
struggling and the tiny lizards scrambling
up the walls. You find her when you're ready
in the barbed wire and fence posts, on the scrub where you walk
with your parched story, where she walks, spendthrift,
tossing up sunflowers, throwing her indifferent
shadow across the mountain. Haven't you guessed?
She's the loneliest woman alive but that's her gift;
she makes you love your own loneliness,
the gates to darkness and memory. She is your best, indifferent
teacher, she knows you don't mean what you say.
She flings aside your technical equipment,
she requires you to survive in her high country
like the patient sheep and cattle who graze and take her

into their bodies. She says *lightning*, and
get used to it. Her storms are great moments
in the history of American weather, her rain remakes the world,
while your emotional life is run-off from a tin roof.
Like the painted clown at Picuris Pueblo
who started up the pole and then dropped into the crowd,
anonymous, she paws the ground, she gallops past.
What can you trust? This opening, this returning,
this arroyo, this struck gong inside your chest?
She wants you to stay open like the hibiscus
that opens its orange petals for a single day.
At night, a fool, you stand on the chilly mesa,
split open like the great cleft of the Rio Grande Gorge,
trying to catch a glimpse of her, your new, long-term companion.
She gives you a sliver of moon, howl of a distant dog,
windy premonition of winter.

Port-Au-Prince, 1960

My sister and I stand at the ship's rail
and watch the Greek sailors
hurl buckets of water on the gangplank.
The drops glow and fall in the bright sun,
here where they manufacture light
and salt air for our happiness.
Next, they unfurl a heavy red carpet which we know
is for us, for our shoes, since our pleasure
and comfort are very dear to them.
All morning, black boys have been diving for change
from splintering rowboats.
I try to imagine how their heads feel
miles underwater where they must swim
to find the dimes. Against the azure Caribbean Sea
their bodies shine . . . they shoot up
like geysers, like fountains of oil, holding one
fist above their heads to signify success. Again
and again they go down to the bottom
to collect the silver coins,
and I notice that they have surrounded us
in their rowboats and canoes, and now they are clapping
and yelling, urging all the white people crowded
at the rail to throw, to throw, to empty our pockets.
Blue-black, they drift in circles, one at the oars, the other
poised to dive, and in my child's mind their screams and whistles
are cries of anger. The great ship inches steadily
toward shore, toward the dense jungle, the golf courses

and tennis courts, restaurants and clubs.
The black boys retreat in their tiny boats,
as our pastel crowd pushes forward. I squeeze
my sister's hand; we have been told to stay
together, to walk directly behind our parents,
to avoid eye contact. Before I step onto the island,
I know that I am different from the people
who live here, I know that I have something another child needs.

Quaker Meeting, the Sixties

Seeing my friend's son in his broad-brimmed hat
and suspenders, I think of the Quakers
who lectured us on nonviolent social action
every week when I was a child. In the classrooms
we listened to those who would not take up arms,
who objected, who had accepted alternative
service in distant work camps and showed
slides of hospitals they helped to build.
On Wednesdays, in Meeting for Worship,
when someone rose to speak,
all the energy in the room
flew inside her mouth, empowering her to tell
what she had seen on her brief
encounter with the divine: sometimes, a parable,
a riddle, a kindness. The fall that we were seventeen,
we scuffed our loafers on the gravelly path
from the Meetinghouse, while maple and elm
leaves sailed around our shoulders
like tiny envelopes, our futures sealed inside.
Despite the war in Vietnam, I felt safer
than I ever would again. Perhaps
those aged, protective trees had cast a spell
on us, or maybe the nonviolent Quaker God
had set up a kingdom right there—
suburban Philadelphia. Looking back, I see how
good deeds and thoughts climbed with us to the attic
room for Latin, descended to the gym for sports,

where we hung from the praiseworthy scaffolds
of righteous behavior. We prepared to leave
for college, armed with the language of the American
Friends and the memories of Thanksgiving
dinners we'd cooked for the unfortunates:
borrowing our parents' cars to drive
downtown to the drop-off point, racing back
to play our last field hockey match. Grim center forwards
shook hands before the whistle, the half-backs'
knee-pads strapped on tight; one varsity team vanquished another.

Haircut on Via Di Mezzo

The brisk beautician nodded toward a chair
and twirled a pair of scissors, one hand in the damp hair
of the woman who ran the milk store down the street
I'd frequented all summer. I took a seat. To wait.
                                               In town a week,
I'd gone for mozzarella, bewildered by the array,
and eager to please you with my choice. I studied the coy
Italian yogurts, their bright letters, milk cartons,
glass jugs of cream. When my turn came, I tried to explain
that I didn't know what kind—*buffalo, misto*—to buy.
She narrowed her eyes. *With whom do you stay?* she asked in Italian.
Surprised, I said your name, trying to frame our friendship and
disguise what I knew you wanted to hide. *Misto*, she said
clearly and repeated your name. *She prefers misto.*
Every few days, when we ran out of eggs or milk, I returned;
she called me *Americana* and asked after you, *bella Marianna*.

Listen, everybody knew everything. At the *lavanderia*,
in the steam, the singing Englishman who washed our sheets
and jeans showed his esteem by chatting with me
about your old girlfriend, said she used to complain
about her shirts. (God knows I'd mend mine myself
before I'd say a word.) In line at the Post Office,
I asked for my mail and got yours. For free, the grocer
bagged an aging bunch of leeks, told me to tell you:
make soup. Nights, we sat on the stoop of our seventeenth-

century home, planned a trip to Rome, struggled to get along.
Only the merchants found our work-vacation amusing.
Between us, conversation had become
a series of sparring gestures.

The eight-year-old rose for her haircut
and siblings turned to stare. On one side of me sat
her brothers; on the other, her parents, and an aged grandmother
dressed for the affair in black. The cutter beckoned
with a long finger, and I saw, suddenly, a rope uncoil
and hair twist down the child's back to the floor.
When the scissors snapped and the first hank of hair fell
to the marble tiles, the girl whirled, the whites
in her eyes flashing. I saw tears bubble
and slide down her face as she fixed her gaze on her father.
Cool and serene, he nodded to her, his youngest child,
and she, obedient, knowing what had to be, leaned
toward the blades and turned her wildness inside.

Family Romance

I

We were still trying to talk about having children—
still believed that talk could hatch an answer each
of us could claim—the night of the outdoor concert

by the female rockabilly group with an unfamiliar name.
Hoisting knapsacks and picnic baskets, we joined the gathering
crowd, couples hurrying to stake out a good square of lawn.

We got enough space to eat and stretch. Then, we took turns
leaving. I made some excuse about going for drinks and stepped
carefully over wine bottles and sweaters, thinking

about the way certain horses under saddle
will gradually work the bit and extend their necks
so that the riders, unconscious, allow the leather

reins to slide through their fingers, until the horses gain
their heads, and bolt—riders thrown, bridle flapping.
Trainers say these horses learn to swindle

their freedom and can be taught to take the bit, to round
their necks, to sense the opening—like fine athletes
everywhere looking for the main chance—and let it pass.

2

Next to us a family from France unpacked their supper
and shared with us their Camembert. They'd forgotten
warm clothes; I offered them our surplus.

First, one accepted a pair of socks; another took a sweatshirt;
Soon, they looked like us in our bright American gear—
parkas and buntings curled against each other.

Like curious relatives from out of town, they were
enthusiastic, generous, but unprepared for the weather, and I felt
protective, wanted them to have the feather vests, to stay warm.

The sky filled with stars, the musicians played, I watched
the French smoke and smile, whispering to one another, passing
a bottle of wine along the row and behind, to us.

Later, when the concert ended, they thanked us and returned
our clothes, and I had a moment of sadness
amid all the thanking, as if now there would be no one

who needed anything from us. Free, I thought of that horse,
too unpredictable for a child, a mount who could fool
the most observant rider. You led the way to the parking lot

in silence, wondering how you would ever have a family of your own.
On the way we passed the French—now all bare legs and arms—
huddled together, a knot of foreign joy in the cold American air.

Peter Pan in North America

Mary Martin, leader of the Lost Boys,
when you flew across the stage in drag,
in your tattered forest suit, teasing Hook,
some of us recognized you. Girl-boy, darling,
you refused to grow into any version
of manhood, while we cheered at the play

in New York, 1960, tomboys pulled from play
to put on dresses and sit among the feckless boys.
Years later, we cultivated our baby butch versions
of Peter before our mirrors. That day, we couldn't drag
ourselves from our seats. "You liked the play, darling?"
our knowing mothers asked. We dangled from the hook

of their question, the answer as overdetermined as Hook's
effeminate ways. Being a boy was best. Second best, we'd play
Peter in school plays, flirt with our Wendy Darlings,
and strap on toy sabers like pirates taking Lost Boys
hostage. After all, Mary Martin could fly, take a drag
from a pipe, dance with her shadow, reject predictable versions

of femaleness. Call it chutzpah or perversion,
we imagined ourselves: breasts bound, hooked
to guy wires, smartly dressed in roguish drag.
We took our own message from the play:
if grown-up, gendered roles awaited all girls and boys,
then woe to her whom he called "darling."

When the time came, we called each other "darling"
and fell into our own problematic diversions
and girl-girl relations. Next door the gay boys
camped it up, swishing around in capes like Hook.
Now we've got adult cult artists to play
the gender-bending game, we know the world needs drag

queens, he-shes, and transvestites at the drag
ball. Behind the hetero scrim, Mr. and Mrs. Darling,
fly erotic creatures of every sexual preference who play
havoc with your repressed aversions.
Skirt and slip, tank and tights, drop the baited hook
and we'll all bite—girls, boys,

everything in between. Drag revealed our own inversions
long before the Darlings were upstaged by Hook,
and grown-up play separated the Marys from the boys.

Too Jewish

You'll be more yourself, my Bubbe argued.
I already am myself, I shouted.
She turned away. *I'll pay!* she cried,
hurling her last old woman's weapon.
In the Depression, her three daughters marched
before the knife, the gleam of good marriages
in her prescient eye.
My sister only wanted a date.

Years later, in Jerusalem, I bought a Star
of David and hung it around my neck.
Why so big? she asked. *The whole world
has to know you're Jewish?*

When the bandages came off
my sister's nose still lacked perfection.
Look, he did the best he could,
Bubbe snorted, always a defender of doctors.
I was their child: half my life
I believed I could fix a problem
by cutting it away. In the name of love
we draw a blade across the beloved's face.

Contradancing in Nelson, NH

for Leslie Lawrence

It was a ragged crew, just like you'd said—
some hippies, gents and ladies, little kids.
On stage, our landlord fiddled in his red

T-shirt, a country maestro, as he slid
his fingers up and down the viol's neck.
The barefoot caller, a local who lived

for the do-si-dos, had a strange inflect-
ion, strange to me, that is. You pointed out
the folks you recognized, oddballs protect-

ed by rural tradition. With a shout
the allemandes began, and a stout man,
pony-tailed, masking a Talmudic pout,

bowed politely and requested your hand.
Couples lined up according to gender
and flew through steps at the caller's command.

The music roused me, summer pretender
to the country life, and I slapped my knee
like the townies who could still remember

Nelson's young years, when locals didn't flee

the Saabs and Volvos racing down the hills.
In cut-offs, a musician tuned his C.

The dancers drank from bottles perched on sills.
We swatted at mosquitos as we looked
at the crowd, noting the women in frills,

the men in funky summer get-up, hooked
on Birkenstocks and silk-screened cow T-shirts.
When the caller started again, you booked

me with the scholar who would have been hurt
if I'd refused. "But I'm a beginner,"
I demurred. He smiled benignly. No flirt,

he explained that in Nelson a sinner
(we dipped past and came back where we started)
is one who can't turn novice to winner.

Afterwards, I thanked him and we parted.
Back on my bench, I wondered: is *she* gay?
When I mentioned the idea you smarted.

"You can't tell by looking," I heard you say.
"These local women defy all the rules.
They're married, ride tractors, and put up hay."

A blond-haired guy asked you to dance, a school-
boy type, a graceful libertarian,
befitting New Hampshire tradition. Fool-

ishly, I didn't ask the fine woman
on my left, afraid to be the only
all-female couple on the floor. You'd been

asked to dance by several girls. A homely-
faced Ginger Rogers put us all to shame
with her sister. Had I only known we

were honored guests, that nothing could restrain
their generous impulse to include
us, I might have found the will to detain

that dark-haired beauty who, spinning 'round, wooed
by someone else, promenaded like a
queen on the arm of a girl, bright eyes glued

to each other. Then up to the mike a
new caller took his turn at the last dance—
traditional waltz; we rose (despite a

brief hesitation) and shot a last glance
at the couples who swept 'cross the floor,
waltzing to the "live free or die" romance.

Midnight Swim

She likes the comely shape of the copper beech
and notes the wedge of sky that shows where the tree
received stigmata. I like to watch her
walk up the path because she is beautiful and
sees beauty where I see sadness: in the retreating summer
night, in the night of the pond's enormous, still eye,
in the amphitheater of bullfrog and treefrog and peeper,
in the silver steam coming off the water, in the arc
of the diving body disappearing, in the splash of a creature
nearing we name turtle or snake. The floating dock
drifts with its jealous reflection appearing like a face.
And I who have no claim on this woman or this lake
take the measure of the summer from the fireflies—
luminous against the dark trees—and the slowly revolving
dock I dream free from its moorings by morning.

Dreaming at the Rexall Drug

In Wyoming, at the confluence
of Clear and Piney creeks, I find myself
watching low clouds mass above the Bighorns.
If I were to get on the bicycle
and ride to Buffalo,

I'd saunter into the Rexall Drug
and order a root beer float, I'd fill out
a contest form to win a thoroughbred,
as I did every week in my eighth year,
in love with the bay in the plate glass window.

In Buffalo, Wyoming, an America
my Russian grandmother never imagined,
we are standing before the cosmetics
counter, and she is testing Revlon
lipsticks to find the perfect shade of peach.

I drift toward the comic books where Lois Lane
is repeatedly rescued and flies—
past skyscrapers and suspension bridges—
as I do in my dreams.
My grandmother takes my hand and we walk.

At the house it's 1955 and
my father has the thick black hair he lost
before I was born. He leads us
to the patio where Chinese lanterns sway
like soft paper crowns. All the neighbors

I will grow to love are laughing and floating
in the buoyant atmosphere, and here comes
my mother in a party dress, holding
my baby sister. I've not yet learned to read
their faces for bankruptcy or grief.

As far as I know, everyone will live
forever, and little girls like me
will continue to win racehorses
from Rexall, where my grandmother will stand,
twisting lipstick tubes, discovering one

imperfect color after another.

Meeting the Gaze of the Great Horned Owl

From a distant room
in the woods
the owl burst down,
flung herself like a skydiver and hovered
above me. I covered my face with my arms and ran
toward her—strange—because
I was afraid.

I had disturbed the quiet
of the feathered one
who rested now, overhead, in a dead tree
where jays and flickers pecked and cried.
The owl acknowledged each note, each tiny, colored movement,
by twisting, on a calm trivet, her troubled head,
the dappled body perfectly still,

and I admit that I wanted
the creature's attention, to compete
with the smaller birds,
so I made my human noises and the owl attended,
turned her brown, comprehending eyes
down to me and met my stare.
I moved my arms—slowly—in an awkward imitation

of flight,
pawing the air like an animal awakened abruptly
or just beginning
to know the power of her wings.
I held the owl's gaze as I swayed
and wondered what she saw:
something large straining to rise

and failing. I thought of my younger sister, dead,
and I wanted her back, to show her,
as I never did in life,
how fear and longing sometimes go together,
how one small percussive surprise
in the trees can turn you
from one self to another, this one with wings.

Yom Kippur, Taos, New Mexico

I've expanded like the swollen door in summer
        to fit my own dimensions. Your loneliness

is a letter I read and put away, a daily reminder
        in the cry of the magpie that I am

still capable of inflicting pain
        at this distance.

Like a painting, our talk is dense with description,
        half-truths, landscapes, phrases layered

with a patina over time. When she came into my life
        I didn't hesitate.

Or is that only how it seems now, looking back?
        Or is that only how you accuse me, looking back?

Long ago, this desert was an inland sea. In the mountains
        you can still find shells.

It's these strange divagations I've come to love: midday sun
        on pink escarpments; dusk on gray sandstone;

toe-and-finger holes along the three hundred and fifty-seven
        foot climb to Acoma Pueblo, where the spirit

of the dead hovers about its earthly home
        four days, before the prayer sticks drive it away.

Today all good Jews collect their crimes like old clothes
        to be washed and given to the poor.

I remember how my father held his father around the shoulders
        as they walked to the old synagogue in Philadelphia.

"We're almost there, Pop," he said. "A few more blocks."
        I want to tell you that we, too, are almost there,

for someone has mapped this autumn field with meaning, and any day
        October, brooding in me, will open to reveal

our names—inscribed or absent—
        among the dry thistles and spent weeds.

Death of the Owl

for Pat Sargent

She said someone will come for the wings,
and snap them off, whole.
Someone for the claw, foot of a prayer stick.
Someone will come for the eyes,
like the woman from Cochiti Pueblo
who replaced her own with the raptor's.
Every part will be used:
the short tail feathers
that cover the arms and torso
of Owl Boy taken from his parents
and changed into a bird.
Nothing is wasted.
No time to stop, I said.
Right behind you, she replied, someone
who needed the feathers of the breast
to place beside the restless child
and induce sleep.
Someone who needed the undertail
feathers for a good peach crop.
I saw the wings lift,
heard the head crack,
no time to swerve—
the bird hunched in the highway
drawn by something dead in the road—
before she hurtled into the metal.
A shaman who required the feathers
for her hair was coming

to gain power over illness,
and someone claimed the remains
of the Burrowing Owl who lives in the underworld
and speaks with the dead.
Someone who wanted an audience
with the Bringer of Omens,
the Priestess of Prairie Dogs,
was coming, she said,
right behind you.

The Roast Chicken

When I set the roast chicken in the center
of the table and sat down, alone, to eat,
I understood the meaning of my life. That morning
when I squirted the lousy Cambridge water
into the coffee pot, I knew why my sister
took her life. The first night I ate
the roast chicken in honor of couples,
in honor of the labor and elegance of compromise.
The second night I ate the roast chicken weeping
with self-pity, because I had no partner to designate
on my health plan form, should I become incapacitated,
my life sustained solely by machines.
The third night I picked at the chicken
and considered how my life has been a flight
from family, and how I've arrived
at middle age without one.
Who will remember with me the old North Broad Street
train station? Who will bike with me to the drug store
in Mount Airy for my sister's medication? Who will know
the hatred I harbored for my father
who could not tolerate noise, and who will love me
now that I have become him, a person
who cannot tolerate noise? Who will ask me
about the Saturdays I wandered around Chestnut Hill
my senior year in high school
with a little money in my pocket,
looking at earrings and
developing expensive taste?

Now I watch my neighbors kneeling
in the early November cold to plant
their spring bulbs. Their faith amazes me,
for today I understand that by such deeds
human goodness is recognized.
All week the brick streets of Cambridge
have been saying *goodbye*, quietly, hushed
by leaves, like a lover who knows it's over
and speaks kindly, finally, in a café
before she disappears. And you're left
knowing that she was your best chance,
though she would say
your best chances are the ones you take.

GIACOMETTI'S DOG

The Problem of Magnification

Today after class, my student explains to me
how he and his roommate plan to trap
history between two enormous mirrors they will install
in space. He is particularly interested in sixteenth-century
explorers, coastal South American countries,
wooden boats circumnavigating the globe.
Kindly, my student instructs me in the development
of laser technology, he persuades me with heroic accounts
of electromagnetic radiation, fabulous as any resurrection.
History, he says, is all matter,
and matter cannot be destroyed. A lasso of light sparks
from his chalky fingers as he describes the problem of magnification.
Today you would lose the fine hairs on Magellan's arms,
the grain in the wood of his mast. Soon, he assures me, technicians
will perfect the lens, the light will refract,
and the boys will see the trees of Tierra del Fuego
as they appeared to the Portuguese commander.
Tonight my student and his roommate elucidate the elegant equations.
Their dormitory room is a planetarium
of faith, earth a lonely place, miles from anywhere,
a penciled circle on the small schematic diagram.

Living in the Barn

for Marianne Weil

Beside you in the truck, I almost forget
you are a woman, thirty, turning the wheel,
slamming the door. You could be a boy, fifteen,
slim and eager for exercise in a soiled shirt and jeans.
By the time you closed the deal, the animals were gone.
but their ghosts raise their heads as we pass.
Black and white cows reclaim the pasture; curious billy goats
eye two women rattling up the drive. Like an archetypal barn
from memory, the barn slumps broad and red in the rain.
Now the great hayloft holds your bed and table.
In dreams, the farm boys bale and hurl their burdens
into the atrium; I feel the heavy hooves of Clydesdales
stamping in their stalls; the walls still hold their scent,
their hairs, their troughs, their significant sighs.

You have restored yourself by restoring this barn—
long days under the sun's hot hand,
hours at the drafting table—
planning for the time you would have what you need:
a place to work, a place to live.
Like barn swallows high in the rafters
your sculptures float and fly, wings beating against weathered wood.
In the studio, your welding tools assume the shapes
of fantastic creatures, the bronze and brass of your trade.
You lace your boots, tie back your hair,
prepare for work like a farmer whose animals,
like a ring of friends, surround her.

The Lover of Fruit Trees

for Henry Sauerwein

The desert of northern New Mexico
stretches behind the garden,
punishing cactus in a hot blue bed.
Civilization begins with the Russian olive
and the Chinese elm.

This year all the trees are full.
Early apricots cluster, and greengage
plums dapple the adobe wall.
We walk what you call your English garden
for its wild and unlikely flowers.

You call them by their Latin names
like the strict uncle who wants to be firm
but loves his brother's children for their flaws.
One blazes bright in the morning and wilts by noon;
another flowers before its time.

We turn to the orchard, your prize,
and I think of the stubborn Jews
who, throughout my childhood, made oranges
grow in the desert. *A miracle*, my father would say.
You understand? A miracle.

Twilight. You reach for your hose
and water disappears into the sandy soil.
Inside, you show me an oversized book
of photographs taken in the Warsaw ghetto
before everything beautiful burned

Philadelphia, 1955

All the lights are on
in the house of my childhood.
A figure passes behind a window.
Then another with busy hands. Someone
is sick. Someone dials
a telephone.

A child in a nightgown
closes the door and walks barefoot
on the black grass. Stars have grouped
like families into their fixed relations.
She welcomes the great indifference
of the street and recites the names

of everyone asleep in the brick row houses.
Pleasure on her tongue, syllables
follow one another into place.
She whispers to fences and mail slots,
to screen doors, to bicycles tossed
on summer lawns.

She sits in the permissive dark,
a guest unwilling to relinquish
silhouettes of buildings, the cold
concrete against her thigh.
Everything that is her own is suddenly here
revealed, separate as her body

from the house with its lights
and troubles mounting the stairs.
Oh wild and tentative solitude, so new,
so graceless. How can she carry it
from the spacious night back to the distressed
and loving people of her life?

The Return

At night he is returned to me—
a small dog with black eyes—
and his tongue stripes my face
pink, the color of his tender
underbelly. We laugh, we weep,
to find each other again.

Cobwebs shine bright as stars
in the forest. I kneel to feel
his fur against my skin, his satin ears,
the fine bones of his skull
returned to me.

In the Sangre de Cristo we run
through paintbrush and columbine.
I follow him into streams where small stones
glitter in his wake. Past larkspur and penstemon,
he fills the woods with his happiness.

When he lies down, I take him in my arms,
a small stillness returned to me, my everlasting stone.
A shovel is waiting. I dig, again, in the dark wood,
as this is my share, to dig and make a place for him
before the light divides us again.

The Children's Concert

Once a month when I was twelve
    and my sister was ten
our mother would drop us at
    The Philadelphia Academy of Music

for the Saturday children's concerts.
    We'd sit in the enormous dark
hall with the other children and I'd
    whisper to my sister

that our mother was never coming back,
    that she'd abandoned us there,
that she was driving to meet our father
    and take a plane to Europe.

My sister called me a liar
    and her eyes filled
with tears. The musicians had started
    on Mozart, but I was whispering

about how we would feel when all the other
    children had gone and we
were left standing in our navy winter coats
    on the grim Philadelphia street.

I did not know then that I would grow
    to love the eighteenth century,
that my sister would take her own life
    one winter day in Philadelphia,

that childhood could be so final a thing.

Riding Lesson

Some days he lurched around
the ring, yelling in Irish. You circled him, he was
the sun, his name was Mick. With his long
whip, he cracked the indolence at your heels,
he made your spine sing its straightest song.

He was a drunk and cast a smelly shadow
while you sat soaping bridles in the tack room
where stirrups took the sun.
Your mother came at six, shafts of light
still hitting the roof of the Impala.

You stood on two hay bales and stared
as they paced in their stalls
wearing bright blankets stained with liniment.
A horse's breath formed a little
white cloud like a man's.

They had the same yellow teeth, the same
lathery sweat. You never knew
when they would turn. At Christmas
your father gave him a bottle, the paddock froze
and the water in the bathtub outside the barn.

After his car wreck, he sat in a plastic
chair and watched the lessons.
With his wet smile. His gimpy leg.
He snapped a crop, he cursed the air,
and then the city closed the stable.

He put the reins of a horse in your hands.
His laughter followed you and made you cry.
Crybaby! He was your first teacher.

Giacometti's Dog

He moves so gracefully on his bronze legs
that they form the letter *M* beneath him.
There is nothing more beautiful than the effort
in his outstretched neck, the simplicity of the head;
but he will never curl again in the comfortable basket,
he will never be duped by the fireplace and the fire.

Though he has sniffed out cocaine in the Newark Airport,
we can never trust his good nose again.
He'll kill a chicken in his master's yard,
he'll corner a lamb in the back pasture.
He's resigning his post with the Seeing Eye.

Giacometti's *Dog* will not ask for water
though he's been tied to a rope in Naples
for three days under the hot sun.
Giacometti's *Dog* will not see a vet
though someone kicks him and his liver fills with blood.
Though he's fed meat laced with strychnine.
Though his mouth fills with porcupine quills.

Giacometti's *Dog* is coming back
as a jackal, snapping at the wheels
of your bicycle, following behind in his
you-can't-touch-me-now suit.
Giacometti's *Dog* has already forgotten
when he lost the use of his back legs
and cried at the top of the stairs
and you took pity on him.

He's taking a modern-day attitude.
He knows it's a shoot-or-get-shot situation.
He's not your doggie-in-the-window.
He's not racing into a burning house or taking your shirt
between his teeth and swimming to the beach.
He's looking out for Number One,
he's doing the dog paddle and making it
to shore in this dog-eat-dog world.

Conversations in July

I

She said three towns away the smell of lavender lives for years
in the workman's shirts, like mushrooms in the trained dog's nose.
I said *here* and pulled some thyme from the rocks.
We didn't say anything. Bats circled in the olive trees.
She loved the broad boulevards of that city by the sea
and the cream-colored hotels. I said *I think my father is dying,
he's turning away from the days of the week, he's afraid to talk,
to give anything away.* She said the living bend
over the counter to speak with the butcher, she said pass me the wine,
she said where are the matches, she said go get some rosemary
for dinner, there is nothing you can do for him.
I said *I want to be faithful.*
She said a river splashes at the bottom of the gorge, listen.
We listened. Finally she said I can't imagine living without her.
Then we imagined it: a stone path leads to a stone house,
a whitewashed room with a small fireplace. A cat sleeps on the terrace.
With a wooden spoon she pushed the garlic across the sizzling pan.
She said I still can't imagine it, so I might as well watch
the figs growing fatter on the trees. We identified a few stars.
Shadows fell on the picnic table as the river at the bottom
of the gorge splashed through our lives.
Someone said go get some rosemary for dinner.
Finally the figs were an echo big enough to eat.

2

She said read to me from the guidebook.
I said, *in the eighth century, elephants and tortoises upheld the sky.*
Griffins guarded sacred trees. The ass played the lyre,
the wolf dressed as a monk. As it should be, she said, go on.
In the twelfth century, the husband pruned his vines in February,
in March he blew on two horns, in May he set off
for the wars, in June he gathered fruit, in July he wore a hat
against the sun, he cut his corn with a sickle.
In August he repaired his barrels, in September he trod on his grapes,
in October he beat acorns from an oak,
in November he killed the fatted pig, in December he gathered fuel.
She said don't forget the one-legged, the dog-headed, the headless
with eyes and mouth situated on the breast.
Don't forget the freaks she said, they were created on the fifth day
and are therefore not in defiance of nature. Go on.
I didn't know you were religious, I said.
Watch, she said and became a fish with a horse's head.
How did you do that? I asked. She winked.
She became a peacock.
I said *this isn't really happening.*
She said you're right, this isn't really happening.

Fable

It was early fall. You rowed me
around the pond
in your ancient boat.
Tart apples lay in a bag with the cheese.
I read you a story
about two women who could not stop
touching each other.
Trumpeter swans paddled close
and you tossed hard French bread
at their black beaks. When you got cold
I gave you my jacket, the leather glistened
like a delicate skin
moving through trees.
You let the oars float
in the oarlocks; you let the boat
drift in circles. You let the women
from the story climb
into the boat. I could not
stop staring. Soon their desire
took up so much room we had to throw
the apples overboard. We had to sit cramped
at one end. Finally we just waded in
and hauled the skiff and the women
to the pier. The story got wet.
The pond was a dark wound.
You unlocked the car and touched
my back, a kindness, as if
I'd always been your lover.

The Bath

I like to watch
your breasts float like two birds
drifting downstream; you like a book,
a glass of wine on the lip
of the porcelain tub,
your music. It is your way of dissolving
the day, merging the elements of your body
with this body. The room fills with steam
like mist off a river—
as intimate to imagine you
pleasuring yourself: watery fingers, slow
movement into fantasy.
You call me in and take my hand
in your wet hand. I have to shield my eyes
from the great light
coming off your body.
When you ask me to touch you
I kneel by the water like a blind woman
guided into the river by a friend.

Birch Trees

From a distance, they are the perfect sentences
we have been reaching for
most of our lives.
They are like the dead

who remember, coming into a room,
how the room grew large
to accommodate
great feeling.

Today in the rain
pale bark unwinds like tiny white flags
and I think of how people
unwrap one another

over a long time and how they learn
the patience to live
alongside the dead who will not speak
and will not go away.

The Subject of Our Lives

The storm has started and they say it won't stop.
Not for you, hanging on in the office after everyone has left.
Not for the ponies in my friend's paddock, huddled and still
and turning white. I know from your voice that you like
this moment—a Friday afternoon, the city between us, a few hours
of paperwork before you can think of dinner or a movie

or sex. I have been thinking about the snowstorm, and about a woman
from Chicago who put me on skis and ordered me to follow her
into the woods. That was years ago, and I've stopped thinking
about her, except during blizzards, everybody powerless and stuck
without milk or cream. Now I see that love is really
the subject of our lives: the authority with which you opened

your jacket and placed my hand, rigid, near frostbite,
against your breast, waiting for the heat to make its miraculous
leap; the gentle rabbi leading my parents from my sister's grave.
The ponies stir at the sound of grain hitting a metal bucket,
carried by a woman who regulates their hungers. How many times
have I confused hunger and love, love and power? My head ached

for years, it seemed, following someone's beautiful back.
My sister wouldn't sleep or wake beside one person long enough to
learn something. *Trust me*, you say, and I'm struck by the force
of your voice, the imperative form of any verb spoken in bed. Come home.
No, stay where you are. Longing will serve us while snow thickens
the sidewalks, delays the subways, tightens every street in town.

BACKTALK

A Long Distance

You disappeared through a tunnel in July;
that was Logan in Boston, my city, a day
when the airport was bright with arrivals.
I lost my imagination,
couldn't picture you once you were gone.
Seventh grade was a large empty map
with the continents drawn in.
I remember Africa:
Se-ne-gal, Gui-nea, Si-er-ra Le-one,
Li-be-ri-a, I-vo-ry Coast.
The rhythms of the words held the countries
& the curve of north Africa in place.
The New York Times says
there is a national strike in your country;
by the time I get an overseas operator,
you're recovering from amoebic dysentery.
I hear my voice clacking over the lines,
& I remember the globe that was a pencil sharpener.
I remember standing in the lunchroom
& trying to figure out
how I could be standing in the lunchroom
& standing on the earth which was the globe.
One night I dream the globe is flattened.
You start climbing north—up to me.
The dream ends with you in Tunisia—
a tiny figure climbing—
until the globe is folded in half.

A Good Education

First, there's daddy, big spender, picking up
the check & mother glancing into his fist
trying to see. She notices the tags
hanging from the dresses, but in the men's
store, he says *one of these & two of those*
without looking.
                        It wasn't fair, who got
what & why. I never knew what anything cost
until it was *too much* or *cheaply made* or *not for us*.
Fractions I never got either, subtracting pieces
from pieces of things. When it was pies, OK,
but when it was point zero zero four,
I ended up weeping.
                           Geometry was the last straw;
they let me out & shipped me up to Latin—
matching the subject with the verb ending,
searching for the missing preposition.
Latin was like long division: once you memorized
the tables, you kept dividing & dividing until
the row was done. On & on the numbers fell
like a connect-the-dots game. As long as you knew
the multiplication tables, the numbers
came out perfectly divided.

                      Next came word problems,
questions of ladders & shadows & the sides of houses.
How did you get the little phrase right up next
to the word it modified, so that you didn't have
the farmhouse marching through the grass but the farmer?
You had to scoot the unnecessary parts up close
to the necessary man sweating through the fields.
                                          Every week,
there were at least six new things every day.
Who could keep up? Laura & Anne & Penny Sharp
were neck and neck; I was the class clown, in the middle,
thank God not at the bottom like Betsy & Suzanne.
The periods were fifty minutes; if it was your good subject,
you wanted it to last; if it was your bad, you tried,
you tried to understand what she was writing on the board,
but you were wishing that someone would throw up,
or there would be a fire drill, or like the day when Kennedy died,
everyone had to go home with her mother.

On Not Being Able to Imagine the Future

Picture the house,
the furniture, the cat,
or you may never have them.
In order to possess
you must envision.
If you fail to imagine your lover
you won't recognize her on the street
when opportunity presents itself
like a bill in the grass.
If you're nearing thirty
practice feeling forty or fifty.
If you don't train
you'll never learn
to play the violin or grow old.
Time will pass
but you won't be able to retire
or plan ahead
because you never planned ahead.
There will be no summer house,
no lake in New Hampshire,
no packing up the car,
no beautiful small children.
A trunk slams,
everyone piles in,
this is someone else's life.

Old Women and Hills

The road to Chimayo
winds
up the mountain
& down
to the fleshy foothills.
They open, pink, like the folds
of skin—
clean, loose, soft—
on my grandmother's
upper arm & belly.
Bubbe, I see you
everywhere in the unfamiliar
landscape.
At Santa Ana Pueblo, three old women
introduce the corn dance.
They shuffle across the plaza,
breasts drooping in black
dresses, chanting in Tewa
a monotonous
drone
like the ones
I heard you chant
over candles
when I was a child.
When they raised their arms,
I bowed my head,
seeing you,
black-veiled,
above me.

Sideshow

It was January,
it was five-fifteen.
I could read the numbers
on the digital watch
I gave you on your birthday.
We were still in that other
kind of time; I could tell
from the way you cocked your head
and because your lips were slightly parted
and your eyes glazed over.
My body hadn't learned
how desire slips away,
how the familiar starts to grate,
and love turns to a passion
for travel, houses,
a few intense moments
between strangers,
to vanity, to memory.

You had another kind of vanity:
the charge of light
by whose grace
the ordinary was allowed,
speech was permitted,
work was advanced.
In every memory of that time
within time,

I break with it, from it,
out into the world
which hounded us
with civic matters—
where love was a sideshow—
but we—freakish,
dumbstruck—helped ourselves
like gluttons to more
and then like patients
on Stelazine
came the long way back.

Prairie

We break off weeds
and put them in each other's mouths.
She slides her fingers
up the milkweed's stem, slits the pod
to watch the seeds float
in the fog beside me.
She pulls me down.
It's the way I thought it would be
when I was seventeen.
The ground is wet. I bury my head
in her chest. She rubs her cheek
against mine—the laws of heat and energy
proven in our bodies.
Here, the illusion of safety—
this is all that matters.
Two women in a field
in the middle of our lives,
while the whole wrecked world
slides into tomorrow.
Her hands come to my body and I would rest
in that simplicity. This field this night
is where we kiss
over and over, clothed, tense.
Before we walk back, she's already walked back,
arranged herself into the familiar fictions.

I remember how she stood among the tourists
the day I thought she wouldn't show,
and we went walking through the galleries
naming the places we'd go: *Étretat,*
Argenteuil, Giverny.

Hockey Season

Maples, willows, sycamores hid the field
behind the Lower School & Meeting House.
We ran in light blue tunics billowing
like maternity tops, cloth sashes looped
round our necks. Elastic from the bloomers
left little marks circling our thighs.
New limestone lines streaked the grass.
        Annie charged
towards the goal; in a year she'd be at Radcliffe,
later in Switzerland studying tree rings.
Past the halfback from Stevens School,
past their fullbacks, both teams
on her tail, she lifted the ball over to Megan
        who flicked it in.
I jogged in the wings, my stick in my hands.
Their goalie tightened her knee pads;
everyone was hugging & jumping up & down;
I heard cheers from the stands; I had half the field
to myself & pictured Corky Miller, who, senior year,
led the team to a winning season,
her grown-up thighs pumping past the players.
She wore the plaid tunic of the varsity squad,
& when I met her on the stairs,
        I had nothing to say.

I recall the smell of the oranges
the mothers served at half time,
the way we sat in a circle talking about the plays,
the stickiness of the lumpy wax we passed around
to preserve the wood on the snub-nosed sticks.
The light faded; we crowded into the cars,
exhausted, clutching our Latin books,
pressed against one another
in the cold November air.

Captivities

I want to tell you that you'll be all right,
but I don't know if you will be.

Long distance, tranquilized,
your words drift by like children
who lose interest in the game
and run home. You lost interest
for years at a time, returned to find
the world altered, familiar characters
relocated, no place to go.

Now I try to call you back with your name,
a word you recognized as you slipped from us.
Doctors. Friends. All sought the perfect formula.

2

I see you growing fat in your apartment.
Outside the light changes; you draw the shades.

At night do you feel hands and chests,
cavities opening and shutting
in the rhythm of your breath?
Do you touch yourself or
is your body a terrifying thing?

Our friends say you eat all day long
like the months between diet camp,
the slimming hostels where you threw
your body against walls and floors, bounced
with your heavyset comrades into town to binge.
Each August you returned—
thinner, tired, ready to start up again.
To eat or to starve, never to leave
the fortress of flesh.

3

I wished for you to marry
a nice man in business or a doctor,
someone like your father
who would take you off our hands.
In this, we failed you. We were your friends,
we believed you needed a custodian
for our fears.

Did I agree that you would never
earn your keep? That you would roam
around New York, cash the checks your family sent,
sit in cheap restaurants all winter?

Your voice drones; words run together
full of blame. And something in me rises,
wants to smack you into shape.
You're ruining the game; you quit
because you're behind
and there was a questionable call
and you never wanted to play anyway.

You're halfway down the street,
yelling, tears falling, and I
hug the dodgeball in my armpit,
scowl, tell the others to pick new teams,
wait for the grown-ups
to call us in.

The Conversion of the Jews

I sat stiffly in the car, resisting
Sunday school & the public school kids
who swore & did it with boys. I went
to a private school during the week,
but in the Sunday school the kids didn't know
anything. Anything. Like when the teacher asked
what the Old Testament was,
I knew it was a source book,
a real history book, but they thought
it was all Jewish miracles.

Their fathers belonged to the Brotherhood
of the Temple & leaned on cars waiting for their kids
to come out with their foul mouths.
Their kids were smoking & touching in the bathroom,
& sometimes the girls peered over the stalls, snickering.
My father bought lox & bagels; it was Sunday &
the table was covered with cream cheese & stinking fish.

On Monday, I'd go to the other school, where
in religion class, Christ was so handsome & young.
Sure, he had more color, more attraction
than those old guys who, though very smart,
were only making history.
We had Joseph with his coat of many colors
& his brothers & the beautiful Queen Esther.

I'd line up all our guys against theirs,
but somehow Christ, hanging pitiful from that cross—
the nails & spikes sticking into his head—
he always won.

I knew I was on the side of the Old Testament,
but the other kids on my side were so mean
I thought of going over to the New. And it's true
I got a little scared in Debbie Lawson's bedroom:
suspended above her bed, a wooden crucifix
with him hanging & a dime store photo of Mary.
There was no way out of religion

until in sixth grade, my friend Annie Post said
Religion was the Opiate of the People.
All those stories, she said—Christ & Moses & Buddha—
everybody had them. Afterwards we had new words
& unshakable beliefs: atheist, agnostic.
Afterwards I felt superior & knew they believed
because they needed to, because they couldn't stand knowing,
as Annie & I knew, that it was really accidents
in space, all chemistry & vapors.

Morning Poem

Listen. It's morning. Soon I'll see your hand reach for my watch, the water will agitate in the kettle, but listen. Traffic. I want your dreams first. And to slide my leg beneath yours before the day opens. Wait. We slept late. You'll be moody, the phone will ring, someone wanting something. Let me put my hands in your hair. Who I was last night I would be again. This is how the future holds me, how depression wakes with us; my body shelters it. Let me put my head on your breast. I know nothing lasts. I would try to hold you back, not out of meanness but fear. Oh my practical, my worldly-wise. You know how the body falters, falls in on itself. Tell me that we will never want from each other what we cannot have. Lie. It's morning.

PERSONAL EFFECTS

November

Of the cold of November this year,
Last, others, little breakthroughs like
Shadows on the wall; twice the number of dried flowers,
Couplets of coffee mugs,
Ashtrays reflecting dimensionless doubles.

Across the evening, a voice
Reflects a memory of that voice.
Someone prepares dinner.
A figure passes behind the crisscross
Of a window.

It's winter. We are walking
From my car parked in some alley.
Back-to-back a fantasy—
That going away,
That coming together.

This city hurries to the shortest day of the year.
We are dogs chasing our tails,
Eating ourselves in the cold,
Eating our lunches and dinners,
Eating books and reflections,
Eating the past, the visions of the past,
Eating the visions of the visions of the past,
Eating the night, eating without end.

A Woman Leaving a Woman

You are setting out from Cambridge
with an old debt
in a brown hat
running like a collapsible umbrella,
a laundry bag of detail slung across your back.

For weeks, you have told me of stirring dramas.
One is strewn with landmarks; years are there.
(He is a man; his life makes sense;
he has come for you; you will go.)

Departure is a striped shirt, figuring
into the crowd, a foreigner checking the maps.

You're carrying it off, sister,
like an exercise in fidelity,
like Indian summer in mid-November.
In a few years we'll laugh, shrug,
but for now,

you're carrying it off;
quickly breakfasting with someone else's children
as if a crime had been committed, and you
were the only witness.

If you return,
if you do not,
if you discover one voice
to satisfy your ache for a chorus,
some morning you will find sandpaper scratching
your memory.

Swallow. It will be your own throat.
Touch yourself. It will be your own hands
serving your own body.
Finally, it will make you glad.

For Bubbe Growing Older

These days, your brittle fingers can barely
lace your corset or slice the apples for strudel.
You curse the God of Abraham and Isaac
Who let this happen.   Age.
Age is the long thud on the door.
Age is stiffness in the morning,
an afternoon's painful walk to the market,
where you cannot reach
the only grapefruit worth buying.

Age is the memory
confusing countries
you lived in, muddling
the perfect stories
I grew up on
and now recite
back to you.

Bubbe, when I was a kid,
we stood in the ocean
at Atlantic City.
You were my lifeguard,
my big Bubbe
throwing me into the waves,
that I should know
how to steer my body
through the undertow.

The Landing

I

Intimate after weeks of close quarters,
warnings of scurvy, beer running low,
they watched the land mass
grow like another ocean
into sand cliffs one hundred feet high.

That morning, no tavern, no public house
received the ship; etched
on a piece of whalebone, it rocked;
scrimshaw designs of shrouds and stays
thrown into calmer waters.

Five-year-old Resolved White gave his hand
to his mother and followed her out of the hold.
Oceanus Brewster, born aboard ship,
had not even opened his eyes, when his father
scanned the shore, blinking back mountains
of twilled cotton and flax.

Leyden had made cloth merchants of them;
a handful of English, ill-at-ease
in the lowlands of Holland, turned
adventurers, soldiers of the kingdom
of Christ, with a Church to found,
contracts to draw.

II

From the shoaling
waters, pebbles
foam with the breakers,
slosh and splinter
over the sandbars
to the foreshore.

If you follow
one grain as it
oscillates
in the swash,
focus on
the small matter
of a single
reversal,
you will lose the grain.

Somewhere, in the back-
wash, in a moment
of tumult, it
returns, over
the bars and
back, over the
bars and back.

III

Dorothy Bradford waited for her husband.
Twice he had waved goodbye, twice
he had returned in the tiny shallop;
he brought tales of adventure at sea,
and once, someone else's harvest,
several sacks of corn.

Six weeks anchored in Provincetown,
she stared at the coast and waited.
Bands of men sailed off to beach on the bars.
Each week brought them closer to winter.

Sealed into the sands of Provincetown's dunes
was her complaint—
that a small child was left behind.
William had insisted. Too good to protest,
too Christian to argue,
she helped the other women with their children,
while the smell of fish—
dead, fresh, decaying—
settled in her nostrils.

IV

They dug at the small mound, pushing
the sand back like dogs
to uncover a bone. Bowls, trays, beads,
a knife, the parcels the dead take
into the ground, they drew and
stuffed into satchels.

They did not uncover
the bones of a sea fowl
but the head and limbs of an Indian child
wrapped in string and bracelets.

V

Dorothy Bradford's Dream

The forest cover gives way. Pitch pines
tumble down the soft shoulder, and beach grass
blows like hair down the broad backs of the dunes.
Two million tons of flash-flooding sand
race into the harbor, seal the ship.
The sand advances. I am a bit of sleeve
On a masthead, falling fast.

VI

Sometime during the third expedition
Dorothy prayed and slipped into the water.
When her husband
returned,
the shipmates tried to explain it.
It was an accident. They were so sorry.
She slipped. No one knew.

The Seizure

When the seizures struck
like a flash flood,
thrust you
storm center, I
screamed in your ears,
clapped my hands that you might listen;
deafened, you stared into the volley.

Behind the curtained air,
syllables stuck together;
all your limbs fell off;
bombarded, the torso surrendered.

I clawed at the straitjacket silence,
afraid that I would catch it
and fall from the day
as I might fall from my bicycle;
afraid of the metals
they hooked in your hair
like hoses to pull the empty places
out of you and onto the paper.

Stowaway, you eluded them.
That passage knew you,
spelt your name, like a flashback,
lifted you day after day
out of the afternoon,
unremembering.

Bubbe 1975

I see you   your red and
white striped beach dress
stooped   walking

slower than
last summer   Bubbe
I see your faded beach dress
blue thongs   straw bag

Can I have a sailor's hat?
Will we buy macaroons?
Is it time to go to the beach?
You dressed us for dinner
and the long evenings
on the Boardwalk

This summer I have questions
no one can answer
Flying higher on the Ferris wheel
lights tinkling   surprises
up   up   in Atlantic City

Bubbe   I've been away
in the woods   and I remember
how you used to say
Mein kind, you have your head
in the trees

Acknowledgments

I thank the editors of the following anthologies and journals in which these poems first appeared:

American Poetry Review: "Late Apology," "Painting Birds," "The Sleeper," and "The Pencil Poem"
The Comstock Review: "Harvey Is Building His Casket"
On the Seawall: "Common Ground," "Eating Greenland," and "Thirst"
Moment Magazine: "First COVID-19 Summer"
Prairie Schooner: "Fortune's Spindle" and "The Hardiness Zone"
San Diego Poetry Annual: "The Walking Cure"
Sinister Wisdom: "Everyone Dies," "The Sleeper," and "You Have to Stay Ahead"
Essential Queer Voices of U.S. Poetry, edited by Christopher Nelson: "Late Apology"
The First Fifty Years: A Jubilee in Prose and Poetry Honoring Women Rabbis, edited by Rabbi Sue Levi Elwell, Jessica Greenbaum, and Rabbi Hara E. Person: "Had There Been a Woman"

For thoughtful attention to this book, I thank the entire team at the University of New Mexico Press. I thank Elise McHugh and Hilda Raz, editors extraordinaire, for wise counsel throughout the journey. My gratitude goes to the friends and writers who read and improved the poems, including Kathi Aguero, James Brasfield, John Daniels, Jan Freeman, Sally Greenberg, Charlotte Holmes, Susanna Kaysen, Amy Lang, Khyber Oser, Leslie Lawrence, and Marianne Weil.

Notes

New Poems

"Had There Been a Women": I wrote "Had There Been a Woman" after receiving an invitation to submit a poem for *The First Fifty Years: A Jubilee in Prose and Poetry Honoring Women Rabbis*. This poem emerged from my thinking about the absence of women in the rabbinate throughout my childhood and early adulthood—and about what might have been different had women rabbis been available and visible. The anthology was published by the Central Conference of American Rabbis Press (New York) in 2023.

The Black Bear Inside Me

"Scottish Melodies": Many regard William Marshall (1748–1833) as the greatest composer of Scottish folk tunes. Fiddlecase Books, founded in 1973 by Randy Miller and Jack Perron, currently publishes *William Marshall's Scottish Melodies*.

Tiger Heron

"Xenia": In the *Odyssey* by Homer, "xenia" refers to the ancient Greek obligation to provide food, housing, and safety to guests and strangers.

Domain of Perfect Affection

"Head of an Angel": From the Durer drawing with the same name.

"The Miniaturists": I am indebted to Willy Eisenhart for his discussion in *The World of Donald Evans* (Harlin Quist, 1980).

"With Two Camels and One Donkey": From a Paul Klee painting with the same name.

The Horse Fair

"The Horse Fair": For scholarship on the life and work of nineteenth-century painter Rosa Bonheur, I am indebted to Dore Ashton, Denise Hare, and James Saslow, whose work informed this poem. Quoted passages are from *Rosa Bonheur* by More Ashton and Denise Hare (Viking, 1981). Used by permission of Viking Penguin, a division of Penguin Putnam.

All-American Girl

"Shopping": In the Southwest, the word "pawn" refers to jewelry or other collectables sold or pawned by the original makers or owners.

"The Crypto-Jews": During the fifteenth century, many Jews in Spain and Portugal disguised their identities by converting to Catholicism or by assuming Catholic religious practices. Generations later, their descendants, having grown up Catholic, discovered their buried histories.

"Peter Pan in North America": I am indebted to Marjorie Garber for her discussion of Peter Pan in *Vested Interests*.

"Contradancing in Nelson, NH": A contradance is a folk dance of English origin, performed in two lines with partners facing each other.

About the Author

Robin Becker is the author of eight previous books of poetry: *The Black Bear Inside Me, Tiger Heron, Domain of Perfect Affection, The Horse Fair, All-American Girl, Giacometti's Dog, Backtalk,* and *Personal Effects. All-American Girl* received the Lambda Literary Award and was an Academy of American Poets Poetry Book Club Selection. A Visiting Artist Residency at the Frick Art and Historical Museum in Pittsburgh resulted in the publication of *Venetian Blue*, a limited-edition chapbook of ekphrastic poems. Her awards and honors include a Massachusetts Artist Foundation Fellowship in Poetry, a National Endowment for the Arts Fellowship, the Prairie Schooner Virginia Faulkner Award for Excellence in Writing, a fellowship from the Radcliffe Institute for Advanced Study at Harvard University, and a Visiting Scholarship from the Center for Lesbian and Gay Studies at the City University of New York.

Becker's poems and books reviews have appeared in dozens of publications, including *AGNI, American Poetry Review, The Boston Globe, The New Yorker, The New York Times, Poetry, Ploughshares, Slate,* and *The Writer's Chronicle*. Textbook authors have selected her poems for *The Compact Bedford Introduction to Literature, Poetry: An Introduction,* and *Serious Daring: Creative Writing in Four Genres*. Among the diverse anthologies in which her work appears are *The Body Electric: America's Best Poetry from the American Poetry Review, The Extraordinary Tide: New Poetry by American Women, The Pittsburgh Book of Contemporary American Poetry, Telling and Remembering: A Century of American Jewish Poetry,* and *Urban Nature: Poems About Wildlife in the City*.

For almost two decades, Becker served as poetry editor of *The Women's Review of Books* and wrote a regular column on contemporary poetry called *Field Notes*. Becker is a liberal arts research professor emerita of English and women's studies at Penn State University and is a recipient of the university's George W. Atherton Award for Excellence in Teaching. While at Penn State, Becker pioneered a graduate seminar in literary book reviewing that launched a cohort of young critics focused on independent publishers. She lives in central Pennsylvania and rural New Hampshire.